Your Story
Matters

Ron Radachy

TRILOGY CHRISTIAN PUBLISHERS
TUSTIN, CA

Trilogy Christian Publishers
A Wholly Owned Subsidary of Trinity Broadcasting Network
2442 Michelle Drive
Tustin, CA 92780

Manufactured in the United States of America

Trilogy Disclaimer: The views and content expressed in this book are those of the author and may not necessarily reflect the views and doctrine of Trilogy Christian Publishing or the Trinity Broadcasting Network.

10 9 8 7 6 5 4 3 2 1

Library of Congress Cataloging-in-Publication Data is available.

ISBN 978-1-64773-516-6

ISBN 978-1-64773-517-3 (ebook)

Contents

Dedication

To Melissa and Matt, Michael, Asher, and Daisy.

May this book be part of your legacy!

Endorsements for *Your Story Matters*

Christianity's roots are grounded in the good news that "God was in Christ, reconciling the world unto Himself," that makes Ron Radachy's new book, *Your Story Matters*, on evangelism and soul winning are so vitally important. We live in a world in desperate need of Christ's story of grace and mercy like never before. The author's work concentrates on reaching this world, just as Jesus did—one-on-one, one soul at a time. I am encouraged and challenged by Radachy's book, as he himself is a shining example of someone who is serious about going to heaven, and to take as many others with him as possible. This is a relevant word for today's Christian.

—Marcus D. Lamb
Founder/President, Daystar Television Network

Ron and Judy have been on the front lines serving the forgotten for decades. This book will bless your life.

—David L. Meyer
CEO of Hand of Hope
Joyce Meyer Ministry

Reading through the book, Your Story Matters by Ron Radachy, I found myself reflecting on my own journey and life story. I've had the pleasure of knowing and partnering with Ron and Judy Radachy for over three decades. Their consistency of faith and life example has never waned, regardless of whatever challenges or unexpected detours may have come along the way. Like me, you will be encouraged, empowered, and equipped as you take the time to read through this timely guide to living and sharing your own life story. Our life experiences and our life lessons become part of our life message, which becomes a powerful tool in helping all those the Lord nudges us to share with. This book is not written by one in the Hightower of theory, but from one who has lived the message. There are untold multitudes who have been impacted by the messenger and the message.

—Doug Stringer
Founder/president Somebody Cares America
and Somebody Cares Inter.

Pastor Ron Radachy has led the way in outreach ministry for nearly four decades. His commitment to at-risk young people and the body of Christ at large has always been a huge encouragement in my own life. *Your Story Matters* is an encouraging book that will bless you and challenge you in your own walk; I know it did both for me. Thank you, Pastor Ron, for your amazing dedication to the body of Christ.

—Pastor Matthew Barnett
New York Times Best Selling Author
Co-Founder of the Dream Center

This is a book whose time has come. My friend, Ron Radachy, unpacks proven, practical help for any and every believer to engage their own world with the life-changing message that truly matters today... the Good News of Jesus Christ.

—Scott Hinkle
Evangelist
Dallas, Texas

Acknowledgement

I want to thank my wife, Judy, for all her hard work. This book would not have happened without her dedication. Love you, Babe!

Foreword

I'm excited to recommend Ron Radachy's book, *Your Story Matters*, to all who have felt the fear of sharing their faith. Starting with his own personal journey of resistance to God and final acceptance of Jesus, he unfolds an inspiring collection of real and even "miraculous" stories woven with a biblical challenge that will give every Christian renewed confidence and enthusiasm in telling their story. This is a great read that grabs your attention from the start along with providing simple (his 2-1-1 approach), yet effective ways of engaging with others while fully depending on the Holy Spirit's help and guidance.

Ron's passion and urgency are truly contagious throughout this book, which he intentionally writes "to dispel fears that have so gripped the Church and rendered them ineffective in sharing the saving grace of our Lord." He puts the good news back into that oft-dreaded word, "evangelism" by removing the guilt-trip many have felt and restoring the joy that is vital in fulfilling the "Great Commission" to which we've all been called by our Lord. While underscoring the significant theological "why" of evangelism, he offers very practical insights about how to start a personal conversation with others that may lead to sharing your faith story. He simply wants everyone to hear about Jesus! Sounds familiar when you consider the Apostle Paul's own request: *Please pray that God will give me his words to speak when I open my mouth so that I can make known, loud and clear, the secret truth of the gospel* (Ephesians 6:19).

—Rich Guerra

SoCal Network Superintendent

Assemblies of God

CHAPTER 1

Who Are These Smiley, Happy People?

It was a cool, summer night in June 1971, a friend and I had just come in off a jetty in San Diego, eyes bloodshot from smoking pot. It was about 12:30 a.m., and a whole busload of Jesus freaks toting their big leather Bibles and a handful of leaflets, unloaded right on the beach. Along came this long-haired hippie type telling me, "Hey man, I wanna' tell you about the best 'high' in the world. You'll never overdose, and it's free..." He began telling me about Jesus.

A friend had given me a light blue Gideon Bible, which was taken from some motel with "Room 104" still on the inside. I had read almost the whole thing and now had just enough information to be trouble to myself and maybe even this zealous baby Christian trying to witness to me. I asked him questions he didn't have answers for. "If God is so loving, why does He let little children die of starvation? Why did He let my buddy get his brains blown out in Vietnam?" I ran him up and down the Bible and challenged him at every turn. Acting very smug, I said, "When you get the answers to these questions, get back to me and we'll talk." Funny... I can still remember that conversation like it took place last week. That was the beginning of God sending the Hound of Heaven on my trail.

I was raised Catholic in Cleveland, Ohio. My sisters went to parochial schools, and I have a cousin who is a priest. My grandmother was raised Roman Catholic in Czechoslovakia and came to the United States on New Year's Day, 1900, turn of the century. She settled in a Slavic neighborhood, and the church she went to was even Slavic, so she hardly knew any English. She literally went to church every day until she was eighty-five years old. She was a prayer warrior her entire adult life.

My salvation probably can be traced back to her prayers. Even at ninety-five years, she would lie down for twenty minutes and be up for five to ten minutes. While she was up and not speaking to anyone, she prayed constantly. I stopped going to church around sixteen years of age. I would tell my parents that I was going to early service and then skip out. In fact, I would go to a local service station where a friend of mine worked, change clothes, and go straight to the drag races. I never saw a prayer answered or saw God do anything I could attribute to Him. Therefore, I saw no reason to keep going to a place that bored me to death.

I joined the Navy in January 1967, at nineteen years old, and left in November of that year. Even at nineteen, I knew that the Vietnam war was playing for keeps. This wasn't a game of cowboys and Indians; people were dying and many of them were my age. I decided that I would rather give four years of my life in the Navy and almost be guaranteed a ticket home than to gamble with my life for only a two-year hitch in a war I didn't understand and might come home in a coffin.

As a jet mechanic, part of my stint was working in a helicopter squadron attached to a minesweeper based in Japan. I ended up going to Vietnam twice.

On one of our trips, we went in at the DMZ (De-Militarized Zone) close enough to watch the waves breaking on the shore, and then began to work our way down the coast all the way to the Mekong Delta. Cruising down the coast one night, while the ship was blacked out (so we were less of a target for shore batteries), I found myself pondering in my mind, *What is war all about? I think it's all based on greed. Somebody wants more than their share, and they are going to take what they want no matter how many people it hurts to get it. And the rest were just defending what was theirs.* On a ship, you have lots of time to think, so next, I started asking myself, *What is reality?*

This started me on a passive search for what was really important. Was it a bigger house, more toys, or was there something more important? Interestingly enough, I started looking for spiritual significance. But I knew it couldn't be religion. I had been there and done that, or at least I thought I had!

I began looking in many strange places to find answers to life. I dabbled with astral projection. This is the ability to cause your spirit to come out of your body and travel around. Having partially done it one time to prove to myself that I really had a spirit. I found no answers there.

I looked into eastern religions. I studied Tibetan monks and books concerning what they believed and their way of life. Many things they said seemed to make sense as to how to deal with problems and people. But through all of this, I came to the conclusion that it was a way of life based on a philosophy of man. This, too, left me empty.

I was a drug user and dealer. LSD was my favorite drug, and I would frequently save an hour or two out of each trip to contemplate my belly button or the problems of the world, but I never could figure out what I was searching for. I couldn't understand what was causing the emptiness I felt inside. I would think and think and think, but concluded I needed more input before I could draw any conclusions.

At one point after returning from overseas, I became interested in Mormonism through an acquaintance. I asked a lot of questions and even went through their classes to become a Mormon. However, once again, something just didn't seem right, and I walked away.

After I was discharged from the Navy in June 1971, I became involved in Transcendental Meditation for six years. I didn't find the answers I was looking for there either, but I got plenty of rest.

At that point in my life and to the best of my understanding, I would have to say that I was agnostic.

In early June 1978, an old high school friend stopped to visit me in California on his way to live in Hawaii. His brother had gone from the wild side of life to not only becoming a Christian but also a pastor. I didn't know it, but since I had left home, Steve, my high school buddy, had become a Christian, as well. During his visit, we caught up with old times, but he was careful not to make his Christianity an issue and become divisive in our relationship.

Several days after he left my place, I got a letter from him saying, "Dear Ron, I've got a job for you, helping me build a house for the summer, if you want it." I called him that night, and after a lengthy conversation, I decided this was a chance of a lifetime, so I packed my bags and caught a plane to the beautiful tropical island of Maui. Little did I know that the owners of the house

I was going to help build on Maui were Christians, but
also the home we were going to live in and house sit
while the owners went to the mainland for the summer were also Christians. I thought, *Oh, blankety-blank
(different words, of course), I'm surrounded by these smiling,
happy, positive people.*

One Sunday morning, a couple and my friend, Steve,
invited me to breakfast. They then decided to take me to
church without telling me first. When they pulled into
the church parking lot, I glanced around to see where
we were, frowned and swore, "No way. I'm out of here.
I'll see you at home."

I took off walking as I grumbled under my breath,
"Who do they think they are? #%&#! They're not con-
verting me." It took me almost two hours to walk home,
and I only beat them by about ten minutes. My attitude
showed that I was mad, so they didn't try to talk about
"God stuff" anymore and left me alone for the rest of
the summer.

The owners of the house we were house sitting for
returned from the mainland. The husband was a skilled
carpenter and joined us on the job. I had heard he was
one of those born-again people, too, and he even had a
reputation that he was a "soul winner," whatever that
meant. He never tried talking to me about Jesus, and
that made me more comfortable around him. So comfortable, in fact, that one day, I felt it was safe to ask

him a spiritual question. He simply answered my question and then went back to hammering. Since he didn't preach at me, I decided it was safe to ask him another question. He leaned through the ladder and calmly answered my question and then added, "You know, someday you're going to get saved."

I rolled my eyes and thought to myself, *Uh-oh. Now I've done it. Why couldn't he just answer my question and then leave it alone?* He saw my eyes roll to the side, and he responded, "Think about it. You are looking for answers or you wouldn't be asking questions. But all your questions haven't been answered yet. One day you will get your answers, and then you'll do it."

And my rational mind thought, *Well, that's logical.* He then turned and went back to work without saying another word. That man made a greater impression on me than any other person I ever talked to about Christ. Not because of his eloquent answers, but that he didn't try to pressure me to do anything. He knew I was still searching.

I came back to California, met a woman who I lived with for a few months until we decided to get married. I have made better decisions in life; this was not one of them. In March 1981, our very short-lived marriage was going down the tubes, and I couldn't stop it. I laid on my bed and called out to God, "God, if you are real, take me and do what you want with me. Just make things right." I remember thinking, *What have I got to lose? Either God is real and can help, or I'm talking to the ceiling. Either way, no one is going to know.* My prayer to make things right was concerning my marriage, but He had much bigger plans.

For two weeks, nothing changed. Then one day in a situation where I normally would have said, "You, G__ D__ S__ O__ B____!" It came out, "Gosh darn!"

My eyes opened wide, and my forehead wrinkled as I wondered, *Where did that come from? What does that even mean? I've never ever said, "Gosh darn" in my whole life!* Puzzled by this new vocabulary, I thought to myself, *What the heck is going on here?* Shocked, even more, I realized I had just said heck instead of hell. This was the first time I heard that "still small voice" inside... not in my ears, but deep down inside, which I now know is the Holy Spirit, saying, "Remember what you did two weeks ago?"

I scratched my head as I said to myself, *"You mean this stuff is for real?"* Since March 1981, I've never been the same. I felt like someone had pushed the delete button to all my cuss words and all my filthy jokes. I didn't try to quit; it was just gone. And I was downloaded with a new desire and passion for a different life than I had been living for many years.

Instinctively, I knew I had had a close encounter with God, the God of the Bible. I really didn't know what it meant, but I knew I needed to start at least reading the Bible to obtain more information. I blew the dust off that powder blue Gideon Bible and opened it up for the first time since I had returned from serving in the Navy in Vietnam, where I had begun my search for truth and the meaning of life.

I started reading the Bible and couldn't put it down. When I realized that I could have my own walking, talking relationship with the God of the universe, I just had to know more. I would get up at 4:20 in the morning, so I could read and pray before I went to work. I read the Bible over lunch, over dinner, and all evening until 10:30 or 11:00 p.m. I watched Christian television when I had time, just trying to learn all I could. God gave me an insatiable hunger to grow.

A month later, I ran into a guy who I knew was a Christian. At the time, I was a building contractor, and he was a wallpaper hanger who had done work for me. I saw his truck in a shopping center parking lot where he was papering a woman's clothing store. He was standing out by his truck, so I pulled up to talk to him. I leaned out my window and commented to him, "Hey, I had a-a-a, I guess you would call it... a religious experience about a month ago, and I thought you might be interested."

His eyebrows lifted in surprise, "Oh, really? Tell me about it."

So, I began to recount what happened. He listened intensely, and after a few minutes, his eyes glassed up as he responded, "Whoa, you got born-again!"

"Born-again? No, I don't think so! What in the world does that mean, anyway?" I smirked and shook my head.

He reached into his truck, pulled out his Bible from his dashboard, and opened up to John 3:3 (NKJV) and began to read, "...unless one is born again, he cannot see the kingdom of God." The word "must" seemed to jump out at me.

With a puzzled look on my face, I sarcastically commented, "It doesn't sound like it's an option? But what does that mean?"

He then turned to Romans 10:9 and 10 and began to explain, "You may believe it in your heart, but confession is made unto salvation. Where are you going to church?"

I shrugged my shoulders, "Nowhere. I don't know where to go. There are a thousand churches out there, and everyone teaching something a little different. Who's got the straight scoop? Where does God go anyway?"

I ended up going to his church, and I wasn't disappointed. Every message the pastor preached at every service in the first two months seemed to be exactly what I needed to know. I felt there wasn't anyone else in the place except the pastor and me. Every message was something that I could begin to apply in my life the next week.

CHAPTER 2

211 for Someone's 911

In 1980, I was a young man who had recently started my own contracting business. Things were going pretty good, and I started making money. So, trying to be smart with my money, I decided that I wanted to invest some of my profit and get it working for me. So, I bought a book on investing and started to digest its contents.

While finishing up a room addition for a doctor and his wife, I had a wallpaper hanger, Chuck Argon, applying his skills to the project. As people do everywhere, we talked as we worked. Since my new knowledge of my investments was foremost on my mind, I began sharing some of what I had been reading.

"You take 10 percent of your profit, and you never, ever spend it, but invest it. Any interest it produces, you only reinvest it, so it begins to multiply."

Apparently, I must have gone on too long. All of a sudden, Chuck whips around, throws his hands out to the side, and says, "Look, man, I'm a Christian. I give ten percent to God, and currently, my bills exceed my income, but all my bills are paid, and I can't explain it." What he said took 11 seconds. I can't even remember what I had for lunch two days ago, but I remember what he said to me in 1980! I even remember what I thought in response, *He's a husband and a father (I don't know what that has to do with anything) and a businessman. He knows what his bills are, and what his income is, what are you going to do, call him a liar?*

That's all Chuck said. I had no response. Christians think if they say anything, it has to be a three-point message with an altar call at the end. Nothing could be farther from the truth.

Several months later, I was approaching a crisis in my life and didn't know what to do. Proverbs 8:1–2 says, "wisdom and understanding can be found where the paths meet or the fork in the road."[1] I was coming to that fork in the road in my life where I needed to make different choices. Chuck's comments were not about salvation but just hearing that God was a personal God who was involved in someone's life influenced me. Hearing that God miraculously provided for my friend was all the knowledge I needed to know to choose Him

---

1 Paraphrased.

versus any other path. Chuck's story has become part of my story. Your story needs to become part of somebody else's story. **Your story matters!**

It's also important to say here, that Chuck and his wife Kathy became my first Christian friends. They were friendly and hospitable towards me until the Lord brought me friends I related to better as a single man since they were married and had five kids.

How could I remember this story so vividly? Because it was anointed to change my life. Your stories are no different than the four Gospels—Matthew, Mark, Luke, and John. Take the direct teachings of Jesus out of those four books, and what are you left with? Stories! Stories of God's Word in action in somebody's life. Your story is God's Word in action in your life and contains the same horsepower to change a life as Matthew, Mark, Luke, and John.

The 2-1-1 Technique is the easiest thing you'll ever do. It's a natural extension of who you are.

2: Two minute (or less) testimony of something God has done in your life.

1: One minute of prayer.

1: One person at a time.

Here's an example of the 2 Minute Testimony portrayed in a true story. I have a neighbor across the street from us. We aren't close, but I officiated at his daughter's wedding several years ago. So we knew each other casually. Every couple of months, we would meet out in the cul-de-sac street and catch up on each other's life. One day I had just come home from work, I was barely out of the car and noticed him jogging over to talk with me. I made it to the curb, and we shook hands. He didn't even say hello, but immediately blurted out, "I've been to the doctor today, and it ain't good." He continued with details of his ailment.

While he was talking, I was asking the Lord what He would have me do. When he finished, I said, "Wow, John (name changed), that doesn't sound good. Listen, I need to tell you a short story, and this is important for you to hear."

"Several years ago, I had what I thought was tendonitis in my left shoulder. I went to the doctor who took an MRI and found I had a torn rotator cup. He didn't even hesitate and scheduled me for surgery for one month later because that's how doctors fix it. He informed me that there would be eight to ten months of rehabilitation. He also said that there is no guarantee that I would have full use of that shoulder again like before the injury. Then the physical therapist told me whether or not I had the surgery, they would have to get my shoulder unlocked. It was a different condition in the same arm. My left arm wouldn't go higher than horizontal. Wide-eyed, I asked, 'What does that mean?'"

"She shrugged her shoulders and casually said, Well, we knock you out, and then we get it loose. My head pulled back, and my eyes got the size of saucers. I thought, *I don't think so!* I decided to take this whole thing to God. I said, 'Lord, I don't want to do this. I'd rather You do it.'"

"The following week, we were having a board meeting. One of our board members was Pastor Gary Greenwald, who has a reputation of God using him for healing. At the end of the meeting, I told him and two others what was going on with my shoulder and would appreciate if they would pray for me. The three of them gathered around me, and Pastor Gary prayed for me about a minute and then stepped back and asked, 'So, what couldn't you do before?' My locked shoulder came to my mind, and I thought, *Here goes.* I immediately raised my left arm, and it went straight up with no pain and has been healed ever since, along with the torn rotator cup." (That happened over seventeen years ago at the time of this writing.)

"Look, John, you may not believe this, but I know God loves you as much as He loves me. If He did this for me, He could do it for you, will you let me pray for you?" And he said, "Yes."

What you just read took me about one minute and forty seconds to say. That's all it takes to change someone's life, possibly forever. No matter what your story is, it needs to end with: "You may not believe this (because if they aren't saved, they probably don't believe it), but I know God loves you as much as He loves me. If He did this for me, He can do it for you. Will you let me pray for you?" This tag only takes about nine seconds to say. It doesn't have to be a perfect match for whatever they're going through, it just needs to demonstrate how much He loves us.

It doesn't even have to be your story. My wife, Judy, has had cancer three times. The second time it was melanoma in her lymph nodes. The Lord gave me clear instructions to have the elders pray for her, which is scriptural. We did what He said, but she still had to undergo surgery. Today she has been healed and clear of melanoma some twenty-five plus years. But in 2019, she was diagnosed with breast cancer. We prayed and believed God again, had surgery, no chemo, and no radiation, and doctors declared her cancer-free two months later. When I share her story, I add a little more of the details to help build faith.

More recently, one of our closest friends had tumors in his lungs that was suffocating him. The doctor said, "It's inoperable, and he has, maybe, three weeks to live. Call the family." His wife and all his friends, including us, looked at each other and commented, "I don't think so." His wife had him moved to another hospital where he underwent all recommended treatments. All of us, his Christian friends, laid hands on him and prayed over him every time we saw him. To make a long story short, in fourteen months, two doctors at MD Anderson in Houston declared him a miracle! Tomorrow we will be seeing another friend who also has been diagnosed with cancer, and I'll be sharing this very story with her.

The reason stories need to be brief is that in our culture today, we have been conditioned to have short attention spans and all the details aren't necessary to build faith in someone. (It has been said that a goldfish has a longer attention span than people today.) However, it still needs to be descriptive. People won't remember chapter and verse as easily as a story. Stories paint a picture in your mind—A video that can be replayed over and over.

One minute of Prayer. Once they agree to receive prayer, find out exactly what they need and pray specifically. For example, a co-worker tells you, "Man, I need two hundred and fifty dollars by next Friday, or they're going to repossess my car." Then your prayer could sound like this:

"OK, then let's believe God for two hundred and seventy-five dollars."

"Why? I only need two hundred and fifty?"

"I'm adding in the tithe."

I'm being a little humorous, but the point is to be specific, so when it happens, they will know it wasn't coincidental. Make sure the prayer ends, "...in Jesus' name." This way, they will know who the Provider was.

One Person at a Time. Let's say that this opportunity happens at work. While you are having lunch, you might hear a co-worker talk about a problem they are currently experiencing, and it brings to mind one of your stories you think would be helpful. After a few minutes, take them aside as not to make them uncomfortable around other co-workers. If they agree to pray, privacy is especially important.

This 2-1-1 Technique, two-minute testimony, one-minute prayer, and one person at a time, is not about walking the streets looking for someone to pray with. These will be people who you already have some relationship with where you live, work, and play. It could happen at your kid's soccer game, PTA meeting, with crabby relatives, neighbors, or Bible study. Yes, Bible study. Many of those who need to hear your story and need your prayer are going to be Christians who are going through tough times or who have drifted away from God and really need encouragement on how much God loves them. That's it. It is very simple and natural to do in your everyday life. I guess I'm giving you the 4-1-1 on the 2-1-1 in case someone is having a 9-1-1!

How to Utilize the 211 Technique in a Church

Now, if you would like to do this on a larger scale, it can be presented to an entire congregation with easy tracking of the results.

You inform everyone that each week in the lobby of the church will be a pan of pennies and a jug with a label on it stating, "People Prayed for Outside the Church." As the congregation files in, if they have prayed for two people this week, they take two pennies off the plate and throw them in the jug. After everyone has filed in, an usher takes the jug in the office and counts them or runs them through a coin counter. In seconds, you have the total for this week. He or she writes it down on a piece of paper and adds it to the year to date total and slips it to the pastor before the offering time. These figures can be posted in the church bulletin, website, Facebook, and so on.

The church can also set up a simple email account, such as; 211@yourchurch.org, and as members get opportunities to pray with people, they can email the church with the short story of how it came about. Then the pastor or some designated person can read through them and pick two stories to be shared at each service. These stories aren't going to contain the end result of the prayer, just the story of how you got to pray with that person.

Now, during the service, at the offering time, instead of the song that normally would be sung, the pastor shares the figures for the day and the year-to-date totals and introduces the two people selected to share their stories. They should have been instructed to rehearse their story and to keep it really short. Containing just the highlights of the story so that both stories can be delivered in the same time frame as the song.

It would be good to keep track of those sharing stories, so it could be a cross-section of the church. Young, old, male, female, new believer, mature believer. These people will become an unspoken challenge to the rest of the congregation. "Wow, if they can do it, I can do it!" Leadership can put pennies in the jar, but should not participate in the story telling time. In the minds of the congregation, they would have an unfair advantage. They have been to Bible school; they're trained, they're anointed. It's unfair competition, the amateur vs. the professional. Besides, this is the means of getting a congregation involved in helping the community.

When a person comes back to tell them their prayer was answered, this would be the perfect opportunity to say something like, "See, I told you He was real. Maybe you ought to come to church with me and see what else He can do."

CHAPTER 3

Knees Knocking, Teeth Chattering... Just Do It!

My purpose in writing this book is to dispel fears that have so gripped the Church and rendered them ineffective in sharing the saving grace of our Lord. Scripture says,

> ...*faith comes by hearing, and hearing by the word of God.*
>
> (Romans 10:17 NKJV)

Therefore, I'm going to do my best to present Scriptures that will set you free from fear, as well as give you the faith to believe God wants to use you to reach your world. And to give you all the practical help I can to make you effective in fulfilling Jesus' last command to the disciples to go into all the world and preach the Gospel. It's called the Great Co-mission... doing it together with Him.

Also, I'd like to state from the beginning that sharing your faith the way I describe in this book is not the only way to do it. The Lord has gifted the Body of Christ with differing gifts. And mine reaches a segment that might not receive the message any other way. It's not the content that is different, but the delivery.

Depending on which survey you look at, eighty-five to ninety-five percent of Christians today have never led anyone to Christ. This fact coincides with the statistic that eighty to eighty-five percent of evangelical churches in the United States today have reached a plateau or are in decline.[2] In North American churches, based on research, more than eighty percent of church growth that is attributed to their size, is transfer growth.[3] That means of the fifteen percent, seven and a half percent are in the same situation as the other eighty-five percent. So, the actual total is ninety-two and a half percent of all churches have little to no growth from conversions of the lost. Therefore, you can see if the body of

2 "The State of the American Church: Plateaued or Declining The Malphurs Group." 2019. The Malphurs Group. 2019. https://malphursgroup.com/state-of-the-american-church-plateaued-declining/.

3 Dunlap, David. n.d. "The Myth of 'Growth' in the Church Growth Movement." Grace Bible Studies. 2020. http://www.gracebiblestudies.org/Resources/Web/www.duluthbible.org/g_f_j/The-MythofGrowth.htm.

believers is not doing their job, churches will not grow, but will decline.

So, why is that? Don't they believe that Jesus really saved them? Don't they believe that Jesus can do the same for their friends and their acquaintances as He has done for them? I believe most believers want to share their faith with others, but the number one reason why they don't... is FEAR!

Most Christians think, *I don't know who to talk to or what to say if I did try and talk to someone. What if they reject me? What if they get mad at me and think I'm trying to jam Jesus down their throats?*

Another reason many don't share their faith is that they realize their own inadequacies. They rationalize, "Man, I know what I'm like behind closed doors, God could never use me!" Most believers do not know who they are in Christ Jesus and, therefore, feel very unqualified to be His Ambassador, which He has called us to be while on planet Earth.

We can't ask someone if they are a Christian and expect that they'll understand the true meaning of being a Christian. In their mind, they think, *Well, my grandmother was a Christian, so I guess I am as well. I'm not Jewish. I'm not a Muslim, so I must be a Christian.* Some think being a Christian is a nationality or your heritage and don't realize it's a personal choice to have a relationship with Jesus Christ. In our post-Christian culture, some have become hardened and resistant to talk or receive information about Christ. This doesn't mean they can't or won't receive it. You just have to take another tactic to connect with them.

Proverbs 11:30 (NKJV) reads, "...and he who wins souls is wise." The word "wise" here is not the opposite of foolish, but defined as "artful, skillful, intelligent, and cunning, as someone who has the finesse to help people understand and make the right decision."

In America, there is a proliferation of preaching of God's Word, some very skillfully, but some not so artistically or even intelligently presented. His Word can be obtained from television, the internet, radio, magazines, CDs, and books. Because it is so accessible to us, it is easy to become apathetic and complacent about our desperate need for the Word and its application for the needs that are all around us. There is a revival in countries where the Word of God is treated like a precious treasure.

What qualifies me to write this book isn't just the training I received from the Lord on reaching people, but also the fact that I never came into a relationship with Him until I was thirty-one years old. The attempts of Christians to try and "reach me" became an education of what to do and what not to do. I know what I would tolerate and what would make me furious, and the latter would pretty much end the conversation.

Something really interesting began to happen to me. I find myself, even now, still amazed by it and a little hesitant to put this in print because some might have trouble believing it. However, it is scriptural, and it did happen to me. Plus, I believe it can help others with studying the Word of God.

In the first two months I was saved, I read the Bible, cover to cover, and was on my fifth time going through the New Testament. One night I took a dinner break, came back to resume reading but hadn't left a bookmark, so I was searching for where I had left off... somewhere in Hebrews. Suddenly, I heard that still small voice in my spirit for the second time, "Who's the teacher here, you or me?"

Instantly, two verses of scripture popped into my mind: John 16:13–16 and 1 John 2:27.

> *However, when He, the Spirit of truth, has come, He will guide you into all truth; for He will not speak on His own authority, but whatever He hears He will speak; and He will tell you things to come. He will glorify Me, for He will take of what is Mine and declare it to you. All things that the Father has are mine. Therefore, I said that He will take of mine and declare it to you.*
>
> (John 16:13–16 NKJV)

1 John 2:27 (NKJV) reads,

> *But the anointing which you have received from*
> *Him abides in you, and you do not need that any-*
> *one teach you; but as the same anointing teaches*
> *you concerning all things, and is true, and is not*
> *a lie, and just as it has taught you, you will abide*
> *in Him.*

I replied, "You are!"

The Holy Spirit then said, "When did you ever go to school and tell the teacher what you wanted to learn?"

I said, "Never. I'm sorry, what would you like to teach me?"

And all I could see was 1 John in my mind. No chapter and verse. So, I turned there and began to read. Chapter 2, verse 3 (NIV), exploded in my mind, "We know that we have come to know him if we keep his commands." It took me half an hour to consume all that He had for me in that verse. I tried to read the balance of the chapter, but it was futile, school was out for the night.

For the next six months, the Holy Spirit became my instructor. I heard His voice daily. I thought everyone learned this way. The subjects varied from day to day, covering a lot of ground. I would come home from work early on Thursdays (which was easy for me since I was a self-employed contractor) just so I could study before

I left for church. I always asked, "Holy Spirit, you're my teacher, what would you have me read?" And I would sit and wait for an answer. I would turn there and read until it was time to leave for church. Time and again, that would be the same material the pastor would be teaching that very night.

Then one day after another class, I felt full. I felt a stirring in my belly that I never felt before. I felt like I was going to explode! And it sure wasn't from any bean burritos. So, I remarked to God, "I don't think I can take anymore right now. You have given me so much... I can't stand having all this information and able to apply it only to my life. I feel like a bench warmer." So, I pleaded with the Lord, "I'll do anything for You. I'll never be happy until I'm in the middle of what You're doing. God, I'll play any position, just put me in the game."

So, I went to church to see what I could get involved in. They didn't need ushers, they even had someone to clean the church and vacuum the carpet. I couldn't find anything that I could get involved with except a handful of Jesus freaks, called *Soldiers for Jesus*, who were going to the streets.

Like a flashback, I suddenly remembered the Jesus freaks that tried witnessing to me. I wasn't very cordial and gave them a really hard time. I was one of those "argumentative types" you probably didn't want to run into on the streets.

Nevertheless, I obeyed and started going out on the streets to get in one-on-one conversations with people. I've got to be honest; it didn't flow like milk and honey off my lips. My first night on the streets, I had to eat three humble pies and swallowed my heart twice. My kneecaps were chattering up and down like a pair of wind up dentures.

Do you know how hard it is to walk that way? I stuttered and stammered and expected everyone to treat me the way I used to treat them. Because right after I got saved, I learned about sowing and reaping, and I just knew I was going to reap a hundredfold return on my hateful, argumentative spewing on Christians. Thank God, those were all committed in a former life, and He wasn't holding it against me. Phew! He said He would put my sin as far away from Himself as the East is from the West. I don't know if you have checked lately, but they don't ever touch. And it doesn't matter how fast you fly; it's always still far from where you stand.

Every night prior to going out, we would all spend an hour in individual prayer and then come together for corporate praise, worship, and prayer before going to the streets. Immediately the Lord started using me. I would see a group of kids standing by their cars at some drive-thru restaurant, and I would go over and start handing out tracts and making small talk, all the while looking in their eyes until I felt a nudge in my spirit and hear the Lord say, "That one is my divine appointment." I'm not saying they all got saved, but when that inner bell went off, they always ended up receiving what I had to say.

In the middle of conversations, the Spirit of God would put statements in my head and heart (see chapter 5) that I just knew were for each person, and the results were always positive. Words of knowledge and words of wisdom became the norm in these situations. The more I witnessed, the more I got used to hearing the voice of the Spirit, leading me in each conversation. We saw people crying in the streets, teens turning away from negative peer pressure, as well as seeing teenage "closet Christians" coming out and taking a stand for Christ.

The first person I remember leading to Christ was an adult male about thirty years old. He didn't just cry, he sobbed, the kind that comes from deep within. His life was broken, and he was ready for Christ. That night as I went home, there were no footsteps behind me. Not because the Lord was carrying me like the poem, but because I was on such a high, my feet just weren't quite touching the ground. What a thrill it was to know that God would use *me* to bring salvation to anyone. The thing I least wanted to do for the Kingdom of God became my lifestyle. When I overcame my fears and knew

I was God's Ambassador, I felt more and more comfortable in sharing the Gospel.

It was probably a year later that Ken, one of the leaders, noticed that we were receiving a lot of first-time participants wanting to join us on the streets. He turned to me one night and said, "You do this pretty well, why don't you put a class together for these first-timers." And I've been teaching evangelism ever since.

God has called each of us to be His Ambassadors. Like any job or position, there might be some fear in the beginning. But the more you share, the more comfortable you will become, and you will be an overcomer of fear.

CHAPTER 4

Power Up With the Helper

We have all experienced feelings of inadequacy and fear. But Jesus told us He wasn't leaving us helpless. Actually, He said, I need to go to be with the Father, so I can send the Helper to each of you (John 14:16). The Holy Spirit was given to us to be a witness for Him.

In Genesis 1:26, He said that He created us in His image and likeness. From the very beginning, He wanted us to be just like Him. But instead, He decided to leave Heaven and come down here to be just like "us". Flesh and bone, born of a woman. But He also came to show us how we were to live. Jesus came to be baptized by John, but John exclaimed, "Whoa, you need to baptize me."[4] But what did Jesus say? No, you need to do this. He was setting an example for us to follow. Then He barely got out of the water and was baptized with the Holy Spirit. From that moment on, the Holy Spirit

---

4 Matthew 3:13, paraphrased.

directed Him in what He needed to do, and then all the miracles began to happen. He was all God, but He was all man as well. He was God with some skin on. He had to be empowered by the Holy Spirit to be able to do all that He did. I am not going to try and bring out every scripture dealing with this matter. However, I will site things that Jesus said and let Him point the way.

In John 14:8–10 (NKJV), Philip says,

> ..."*Lord, show us the Father, and it is sufficient for us.*" (...) "*He who has seen Me, has seen the Father.*" (...) "*I do not speak on My own authority*, but the Father who dwells in Me *does the works.*"

> "*Most assuredly, I say to you, he who believes in Me, the works that I do, he will do also, and greater works than these he will do, because I go to My Father.*"
> (John 14:12 NKJV)

Now the word "believe" in this verse is the Greek word "pisteuo," which indicates a committed relationship with Him. Verses 13 and 14 He says, "Ask me anything and I'll do it for you." Now this is the first two verses out of six times in these three chapters where He essentially repeats this same statement, ask Me and I'll do it that the Father will be glorified in the Son.

"If you love Me, keep my commandments. And I will pray the Father, and He will give you another Helper, that He may abide with you forever. The Spirit of Truth, whom the world cannot receive..."

"But the Helper, the Holy Spirit, whom the Father will send in My name, He will teach you all things, and bring to your remembrance all things I have said to you."

(John 14: 15–17, 26 NKJV)

Wait for Him. He's coming!

Now Jesus just got finished telling them that He will be leaving soon, and they're freaking out.

"Nevertheless I tell you the truth. It is to your advantage that I go away, for if I do not go away, the Helper will not come to you; but if I depart, I will send Him to you. And when He has come, He will convict the world of sin (...) because they don't believe in Me."

(John 16:7 NKJV)

The balance of verse 16 is a much fuller explanation and description, I encourage you to read all of it, but for this moment, it's sufficient. Wait for Him!

Then there's the Lord's prayer. Not Our Father who art in heaven..., that's Jesus teaching us how to pray.

John 17 is Jesus praying aloud because He wants His disciples to hear this prayer. I just want you to see these couple of verses in John 17:20–21 (NKJV):

> "I don't pray for these alone, but also for those who will believe in Me through their word; that they all may be one, as You, Father are in Me, and I in You; that they also may be one in Us..."

How can we be one with them without the Holy Spirit? He's not threatened that you would be "like" Him. That's been His intention all along.

Acts 1 describes when Jesus is about to ascend into Heaven. Jesus probably had many kind things to say to His mom, Mary. Fist bumps and hugs to His apostles. However, none of that was recorded here.

Jesus instructs them with what was undoubtedly, the most important matter.

> And being assembled together with them, He commanded them (italics are mine; not a suggestion) not to depart from Jerusalem but wait for the Promise of the Father, "which," He said, "You have heard from Me; for John truly baptized with water, but you shall be baptized with the Holy Spirit not many days from now."
>
> (Acts 1:4–5 NKJV)

Verse 8 (NKJV) gives further instructions,

> *"But you shall receive power when the Holy Spirit has come upon you; and you shall be witnesses to me in Jerusalem, and in all Judea and Samaria, and to the end of the earth."*

Wait for Him! He's coming soon! Wait for Him!"

> *And they were all filled with the Holy Spirit and began to speak with other tongues as the Spirit gave them utterance.*
>
> (Acts 2:4 NKJV)

This was the day, the moment when the New Testament Church was birthed... birthed with the Holy Spirit and speaking in tongues. Signs and wonders right out of the gate. Now read the subsequent verses carefully. It does not say they spoke in all these other languages; that wouldn't be a surprise since "those dwelling in Jerusalem" at that time were from all different countries, but they each *heard* in their own language. And what did they hear? "...we hear them speaking in our own tongues *the wonderful works of God*" (Acts 2:11 NKJV). They were already witnessing to them.

Verse 12 poses a question "...whatever could this mean?" They thought they were drunk, but Peter says,

"Nay, nay!" and starts to quote the prophet Joel, an ancient prophesy describing this day and what was to come. Then Peter immediately starts telling them about Jesus, who He was and what He did. So, when he finishes preaching to them, scripture says they were "cut to the heart" and asked, "Men and brethren, what shall we do?" (Acts 2:37 NKJV).

> *Then Peter said to them, repent and let every-one of you be baptized in the name of Jesus Christ for the remission of sins; and you shall receive the gift of the Holy Spirit.*
>
> (Acts 2:38 NKJV)

Now I know that there are churches and whole de-nominations that believe all the signs and wonders have passed away with the apostles. Why would God give Joel this prophecy, and Jesus kept exhorting the disciples, "Wait for Him, wait for Him, He's coming, wait for Him?" Why would God birth the church in this manner to cause us to be just like Jesus and then have His power fade away with this first group?

Acts 2:39 (NKJV) lays all that to rest.

> *For the promise is to you and to your children, and to all who are afar off, as many as the Lord our God will call.*

This statement isn't relational, it is chronological. Now, we, the Church, are the new headache for the devil. Just like Jesus, and we are all over the world! Words of knowledge, words of wisdom, healings, signs, and wonders to get the attention of those who don't have a relationship with Him. You don't have to wait any longer, be filled with His Spirit!

Wasn't it amazing everything Jesus did while on the Earth? But not everyone got to see Him do these things, they just "heard" the stories. He's still moving today, and it's "these" stories that will build faith and cause people to want what He can do. Once again, our authority releases His ability.

The baptism of the Holy Spirit isn't just for witnessing and signs and wonders, but for our personal growth, to be our Guide, our Counselor, and our Helper in everything we do.

CHAPTER 5

The Nudge

One night, while well into a conversation with a young man about sixteen-years-old, I heard one word in my spirit (not my ears). "Forgiveness" was the word, and it came so loud that I stopped in mid-sentence to contemplate it. While wondering where that had come from and what I was supposed to do with it, I looked up and noticed that this kid was staring at me with eyebrows raised and a questioning look on his face, which prompted me to continue where I had left off.

Moments later, I heard it again. This time I knew it must have been the Spirit of the Lord nudging me. I didn't abruptly change lanes, but wrapped up what I was talking about and then transitioned into talking about forgiveness. Why was it only one word? Shouldn't the Spirit have told me everything to say? He knew my way of explaining forgiveness would be sufficient for Him to work within this young man's heart.

Within minutes of talking about forgiveness, this young man's eyes started to well up with tears, but he was too proud to cry in front of me. As it turned out, he had been busted on drug charges and put in a juvenile hall where he was saved through someone with a ministry there. He got out and started hanging out with the same people and doing the same dumb things that had him thrown in there in the first place. He felt that he had lost his relationship with the Lord or was well on his way, and he was devastated at the thought.

Had I continued along with my agenda and not listened to the leading of the Holy Spirit, I would have missed what this young man really needed to hear. This young man rededicated himself to the Lord. I ministered to him about God's forgiveness and forgiving himself, which is what he really needed to do to keep his relationship with Jesus alive.

Many of us have witnessed the move of God in church services. We understand that the power of God on earth today is the Holy Spirit. Should we only look for Him to move in our churches, or do we need to look to Him for leading and direction wherever we go and in whatever we do outside of church in our daily lives? Some of the greatest moves and miracles of God, both in the four Gospels and the book of Acts, as well as in the world today, have happened outside the walls of the Church. He is called our Helper and our Counselor.

When the Spirit of God speaks inside of us, I like to call it, "The Nudge". He can speak to us in any number of ways. It could possibly be only one word, short statements, or whole paragraphs. It could be an impression or a picture in your mind. No matter how He shows up, He'll only show up if He is needed. You don't have to make an announcement, "The Holy Spirit just spoke to me about you!" Just follow His leading and watch Him work. Don't expect to hear some booming voice in your ears, but subtle nudges in your spirit. He will surprise you in ways you don't expect and can show up when you are not even looking for Him. He could give you statements that you never even thought of before or give you some of the greatest wisdom of your life. It could result in miracle healings, deliverance, or some other demonstration of the power of God. He will only speak up as needed to take advantage of the opportunity to make a difference.

Other times, He may give you whole statements. There were two Christians in a heated discussion with a Muslim, not long after 9/11. They argued back and forth many times and didn't seem to be making any headway. All of a sudden, one of the Christians firmly declared, "You know the difference between your god and our God? Your god requires you to die for him! Our God already died for us." As soon as he said that statement, he thought to himself, *Wow, that was good. Where did that come from?* I said, "Yea, that was good, where's my pen. I want to write that down." These guys said that two minutes later, the conversation was over. The Muslim had no response. How will this revelation affect his theology?

Another case in point happened between a Jewish man and myself. I used to have lively discussions concerning religion with him. He was highly educated and taught in his synagogue. He challenged me many times and made me prove everything I said. He was the kind of guy that if I made one statement, he would talk for ten minutes.

One day while talking to a friend of his, the Spirit of God gave me a word I knew was for him. I turned and called to him, "Oscar, look up. The sky is clear, and the sun is shining. That's reality. Whether or not you agree with the fact that the sky is clear and the sun is shining is irrelevant. It's the same way with God; whether or not you accept the fact that the Messiah has already come doesn't change a thing." He looked at me with a little smirk on his face like he was going to say something, but looked away. It was the first time he had no response because he couldn't prove me wrong. I don't know the end of Oscar's story, but I did see him about a year after this encounter, and he told me he left his synagogue. "You left? Why?" I asked.

"Because I told my Rabbi that I was studying the life and teachings of Jesus."

The Rabbi said, "You can't do that!"

Oscar replied, "Don't tell me what I can and cannot do! So I left."

I put my hand on his shoulder, smiled, and said, "You know Oscar, because of your diligence to study and your determination to know the truth, one day you will become a completed Jew."

He asked, "A completed Jew, what's that?"

"One who has come to the conclusion that Jesus is the Messiah. And when that happens to you, there won't be a Jew on the face of the earth that you will not be able to convince that the Messiah has come."

He looked at me with that same little smirk, like he was about to say something, but again nothing, he couldn't prove me wrong.

There have also been times when the Lord gave me "Words of Knowledge," information about people that I couldn't have known any other way. Sometimes you use this information to structure the conversation in such a way as to minister to their particular need. Other times you just tell them what you know. When they want to know how you knew that, you respond with, "The Lord has shown me this to let you know that He knows what you're going through and that He loves you too much to let you go through it alone, so He sent me to minister to you." They are shocked that you know personal information, but to the lost, it is a sign and a wonder that cannot be ignored. From this point on, you will have their undivided attention.

One time the Lord gave me a two-part understanding of a man I met at Mardi Gras in New Orleans. He was probably in his mid-forties and walked up with two of his buddies, each holding fresh forty-ounce beers in their hands. As we talked, he indicated that he didn't go to church anymore, but his brother had been his pastor. Then the Lord gave me "the Nudge".

I began to tell him what was going on in his life; things about his relationship with his brother and his relationship with the Lord. I was not speaking like someone who had been reading his mail, but more like someone who had been sitting in his living room.

He looked a little stunned and quietly said, "Wow, you're good."

I said, "That's nothing, now let me tell you what He wants to do with you."

I proceeded to give him a prophetic word the Lord gave me. As I did, his eyes started to well up, and when I had finished, he looked down at his beer and threw his new, big $10 beer right into the gutter.

First, the Lord had to get his attention and let him know that He knew why he had left the church and that he didn't have a problem with God. Then I encouraged him with the fact that God wanted to use him in the future. I was just the messenger boy.

While out overseeing the teams on the street one night with my friend, Ken, he shouted, "Quick, pull in here." It was a strip mall with a 7-11, a couple of stores closed for the evening, and a laundromat. Ken immediately engaged someone in conversation. As I began to look around, I noticed a lady sitting in her car, waiting for her son to come out of the store. He got in the car, and they left. I proceeded into the laundromat, ministered to a lady, and led her to the Lord. As I came out and went back by 7-11, the same lady in the car came back, and her son went back into the store. This time as I looked at her, the Lord gave me knowledge about her. I walked up to her open window and said, "Your husband has left you. And out of your loneliness, you're sleeping around looking for affection." She looked up at me with shock on her face and burst into tears. You see, she belonged to God; she was backslidden. I ministered to her quickly without having to embarrass her in front of her son, and she received it. Even after her son got back in the car, I continued because the most embarrassing information was already out. She recommitted her life to the Lord that night.

Sometimes we hear stories about a move of God, and we wonder if it really happened the way we heard it told. I think it's just human nature to wonder if the story has been exaggerated, even just a little bit. And when we hear these stories, it's always the other guy that it happened to. Well, now I have gotten to be the other guy.

Judy, my wife, our two kids, and I had gone to New York City to help in an outreach, organized by Ricky and Arlene DelRio. It was called *Jesus Loves You, New York*.

One of the events in this outreach was an evangelistic concert to be held in Bryant Park on forty-second Street. We had spent several hours passing flyers around town before the event started. When we returned to the park, I observed three ladies involved in the outreach standing together and talking. A rather intoxicated male, about forty-five-years-old, started pestering the ladies. I don't know how drunk he was, but let's just say he was one drink past the point of no return. He was really beginning to annoy them in his drunken stupor. So, as he took a step closer, I stepped in between the ladies and him and motioned to him to go away. I didn't try to witness to him, knowing how hard it can be trying to reason with someone under the influence. He responded to what I said, but I couldn't hear his response because the band had already begun to play. So, I leaned in closer and said, "What did you say?" When I realized that he was speaking in a foreign language, I thought, *What have I got to lose, he's half drunk*. So, I called out to God and said, "Lord, give me the gift of tongues that I can talk to this guy."

When he finished talking, I began speaking in my prayer language, directing my statements to him. After about twenty to thirty seconds, I stopped, and he began to respond to me as if he understood everything I just said to him.

So, when the guy stopped talking, I started again. This time I threw in a few hand motions and a few facial expressions, not having the slightest clue what I was saying to him. We carried on this conversation like this for almost five minutes. Then I finally said something that he apparently didn't agree with. He was frowning as he waved his hand and said, "No, no, no." Then he turned and began walking away.

I stood staring at him for a moment as he walked away, scratching my head, and thought, Whoa, what just happened? I turned around to the three ladies, and I just shrugged my shoulders. One of the ladies leaning against a car, said, "It sure was good that you could speak Ukrainian and be able to talk to him."

"Ukrainian? You heard Ukrainian?" I quizzed as I laughed out loud.

She said, "Yea, don't you speak it?"

"No, lady!" I'm in shock now and declared dogmatically, "Not a word!"

"No, no," she said, "You must because you used all the slang terms, too."

We both stared at each other and almost simultaneously said, "Whoa!"

She told me Ukrainian was her first language because her parents escaped Russia before World War II. So, I asked her what I was saying to this guy, and she said, "I couldn't hear too clearly because of the band, but you were definitely telling him about the Lord."

Twenty-something years later, I was at a conference in Texas, and this same lady came up to me and recounted the story just exactly as I had remembered it, which gave me a boost in my faith.

Miracle healings are as possible as any other gift during witnessing. Jesus performed many miracles out on the streets, in the synagogues, and in people's homes. You can really operate in the same gifts. Jesus said we could do even greater things than He did.

Years ago, when I was still with *Soldiers for Jesus*, we were based out of San Bernardino, California. We were more radical than most and would often frequent places the average Christian wouldn't even consider going into.

One event that we would evangelize every year was Old Miner's Day in the mountain resort of Big Bear. We had participated in parades, passed tracts to crowds along parade routes, and talked to people picnicking in the parks. But one of the interesting places we would go to was a biker bar called Chad's. Outlaw Biker Clubs used to hang out there. Even though they looked tough and their language was very crude, they really weren't hard to talk to, so we would even take women into this bar to witness to these guys. We would put a quarter on the pool table; then, the bikers would have to play us while we engaged them in conversation.

Sondra Berry Young and Diane Geyer had approached a guy sitting on his bike talking with friends. They started small talking with him when one of them noticed that he had a reinforced leather support on his left wrist.

One of the women asked him, "What is wrong with your wrist?"

He replied, "Ah, I had a bad motorcycle accident and mangled my wrist, and it never healed right, so I have to keep this brace tightly laced to be able to use my hand."

After much discussion, they convinced him that the Lord could heal it.

They reached out to grab his arm, "Can we pray for your wrist?"

At first, his eyes were closed, but suddenly they popped open, and he started staring at his wrist and moving it around as he shouted, "It's burning!" They assured him it was God's Spirit doing this. When they were done praying, he exclaimed, "It ain't hurtin' anymore!"

Without them telling him, he unlaced the brace and removed it. He began making circular motions with his hand and kept shouting to his friends, "There's no pain." Giggling and crying like a girl, he kept repeating, "It doesn't hurt anymore." Then he started going from friend to friend crying and telling them, "Dude! God just healed me. Look, I can move my wrist!" That miracle encouraged him so much that he gave his life to Jesus.

This true story demonstrates two things. Most people think that those with a tough image are unapproachable. Not true, they have the same needs as the rest of us. And secondly, all the Lord has to do is touch the right person and he'll tell the world of the goodness of God and prepare the way for us to minister. There is no way of telling how many lives will be changed by one miracle.

One year on New Year's Eve, I was in Pasadena, California. People come two days before the Rose Parade just to homestead a piece of curb for the best view possible. I had been witnessing with two partners when I had struck up a conversation with three teenage girls about seventeen-years-old. It was a textbook example of how a conversation should go. I got to use my best examples and analogies. They were hanging on every word and so hungry for each statement. As I was bringing the conversation to a close, there was no question in my mind that I was going to ask them to pray with me. Then all of a sudden, I hear that still small voice on the inside say, *"Don't ask them to pray."*

Without any hesitation, I began to say, "Well, ladies, it's getting late, we have to get going. It's been really nice talking with you. I hope you all have a wonderful new year." I shook each of their hands, and we left. Even my partners couldn't believe that I didn't even make an offer to pray with them.

About an hour later, we were walking down Colorado Boulevard on the other side of the street. My partners and I were giving out leaflets about Jesus along the curb when someone grabbed me around the neck and started hugging me. I couldn't see who it was until they let go of me. It turned out to be one of the three girls, and the three of them hugged the three of us. When the last one finished hugging me, she was wiping mascara from under her eyes and explained, "We just wanted to thank you for all the things you shared with us. It really got to us." I tried to say, "You're welcome," but could hardly get it out for the lump I was feeling in my throat.

Could it be that, maybe, they grew up in Christian homes and their parents were pushing a relationship with Jesus on them? And maybe they were having a tendency to reject it until our conversation? I don't know, but one thing I feel confident about, if I had not listened to the leading of the "Nudge," I could have missed meeting their need.

Sometimes our sharing with someone can be breaking up hard soil and removing boulders. It might be digging up the soil. Or planting seeds in prepared soil. Or maybe watering the seed or being sunshine to the "spiritual new plant." Sometimes we are fertilizing the work God has already begun in their heart. Maybe we are pruning some bad theology or concepts about God. Then sometimes we get to be the Harvester. But we should always be sensitive to the "Nudge" from the Spirit as to what God is doing in that person's life.

CHAPTER 6

How Do I Start the Conversation?

On the night of the Las Vegas massacre, we had just returned home. I remember feeling the need to check a little notebook I keep in our car detailing oil changes and the like because I do our vehicles on my own schedule. I was shocked to see that we were overdue for an oil change. I am *never* late for an oil change.

The next day was our day off, and my wife and I had a full list of things we planned to do that day. I told Judy I would go and get the oil changed early in the morning, and we would still get everything done. I took a little homework with me that I finished up in the waiting room, then came out to check on our car. As I positioned myself to where I could see into the bay, it put me within earshot of another customer who was on the phone. He was telling someone that his two cousins were at the Vegas concert, and no one had heard from either one, and the family was very worried. I could not help but glance at him, and he knew I was listening. When he hung up, I knew I needed to say something.

"I can't think of a time that people need Jesus in their life more than now. You're not safe anywhere." I said. "You're not safe at the mall, a movie theatre, church. You're not even safe in your own home. If you're the recipient of a stray bullet, you better know God."

I hesitated and then thought, *That's enough for now.*

"And I have walked away from God," he responded.

I immediately stopped in my tracks and asked, "Really? Why?"

He got really uncomfortable, and I could tell he was apprehensive about telling me why.

"Look, man, I can't think of a safer situation than this. We don't know each other, and we'll probably never see each other again."

He began to explain. "You see, I was raised by my grandmother. She's a good woman. I am married now and have kids of my own. Well, we got into an argument a couple of months ago, and she started to hit me. Then the hits turned to punches. She wouldn't stop; I lost my temper and hit her back!" He was very distraught but continued. "She didn't deserve that, and I not only can't forgive myself, God probably hates me too."

I responded with this story. "Listen, Julio, I met a guy once who used to be a hitman for the Mexican mafia. He killed people for a living. Today, he's a minister. Who would be forgiven more, you or him?"

He instantly responded, "He would."

"Well, if God forgave him, don't you think He would forgive you? Look man, don't run from God. Run to Him and ask Him to forgive you. And go to your grandmother and do the same. I'm sure it will be ok." He nodded in agreement.

Right then, I was just overwhelmed by emotion and said, "Man, I want to pray for you so much right now."

Without hesitation, he said, "Would you please?"

So, right there in the oil change parking lot, I was praying for a brother that lost his way and needed help from the family of God.

When I got home, I pulled out my little notebook to update the next oil change. IT WASN'T DUE FOR ANOTHER 1,000 MILES. Thank you, Lord, for the divine appointment!

Knowing how to start a conversation is everyone's single biggest challenge. So, I'll begin with scriptural references, and then I'll give you some of my own lines that I find work well only to get you started, then you'll have to add some of your own. There is not just one way to start a conversation with someone since most conversations about the Lord didn't begin there, only transitioned there. That is the art, how to transition from any subject into issues that Christianity can be of help.

Jesus gave us an example in John 4 of how He started a conversation. He was sitting at Jacob's well (the local Starbucks in that day) when a woman comes to draw water. He opened the conversation with a very natural line, "Excuse me ma'am, could I have a cup of water, please?"[5]

She looked over her shoulders to see if anyone was watching. She was shocked because a man was talking to her in public. She responds, "What? You want water from me? Since when do you Jews want anything from a Samaritan?" Jesus turned the conversation from natural to things of the spirit.

"Ma'am, if you had my water, you would never thirst again!"

"What water? You don't even have a bucket, how are you going to get water out of this well? Who do you think you are? Do you think you are greater than Jacob, who gave us this well?"

I don't know about you, but I can imagine this little woman running off at the lip.

Let me dissect this story a little bit, and let's see if we can get a glimpse of what Jesus was doing. First, Jesus talked to a Samaritan woman. In those days, Jews really had no dealings with Samaritans, if they could help it. Second, He was talking to a woman. There was a strict separation between men and women in those days that

---

5 My translation.

made this encounter even more unusual. Didn't Jesus know that the Jews had no dealings with the Samaritans? Of course, He did! So, He used it as leverage at the start of the conversation, knowing that just talking with her would get her undivided attention.

Next, He entices her further by making the statement, "If you had My water, you would never thirst again." Now think of the elements of that statement. Here He is standing empty-handed, asking her for a drink and talking about His water. What kind of water could this be that you would never get thirsty again? Not even Gatorade can make that claim! He makes a statement that causes her to ask Him questions. If any time during this conversation, she says, "I don't want to talk about this anymore." His response could become, "I didn't start this, you asked Me a question, and I was simply answering you."

Jesus baited her into this conversation. He has called us to be a fisher of men, and anyone who has ever done any fishing knows that it takes different bait to catch different fish. Not only different bait, but also there are different techniques in hooking and skills in keeping the fish on the line. In Proverbs 11:30 (NKJV), it says, "...He who wins souls is wise." The word wise in this context isn't the opposite of foolish but means finesse or skilled. You don't want to be "pushy" to "catch your fish," they may break the line and swim off.

Then Jesus gets a word of knowledge concerning this woman at the well. If you notice, He doesn't beat her up with this information or to start piously proclaiming, "Thus says the Lord you are an adulterer and living in sin..."[6] He uses this bit of knowledge to spice up the conversation with her.

"I tell you what, go get your husband, and we'll talk more."

"I'm not married."

"Yes, you're correct. You have had five husbands, and you're shacking up now."[7]

She goes back to town, and if you notice, she goes not to just one person but to a whole bunch of people, and says, "Some guy told me everything I've done in my life." It might be a little exaggerated, but the conviction of the Holy Spirit was all over her, so she felt like He knew everything about her. The impact of this conversation opened the door not only to share with her but the whole town. And not just for a few hours, but several days.

For many years we have had thousands from all fifty states come to Hollywood and make week-long mission trips. The Hollywood Mission Trip trains students and then gives practical opportunities to put into practice what they have just learned. Before the teams go

6 Paraphrased.

7 My modern translation.

out, we have them wait on the Lord for a few minutes to see if God speaks to them about anyone in particular that He wants to make a divine connection with or if He gives them a picture in their mind of someone. Sometimes He speaks to their spirit about a piece of particular clothing or accessory items to help identify them. Sometimes they may even get a name or a condition they are facing. I describe this as "The Nudge" in the previous chapter. This happens quite often, and the teams get to be God's Ambassadors, representing the Kingdom of Heaven.

One night on Hollywood Blvd, we had a team from *Christ for the Nations* sharing Jesus with people. There was a family who had "accidentally" ended up in Hollywood instead of going to the beach. Now those are opposite directions, so you have to know that it was no accident. One of our students got "the nudge" from God for the husband, who had just been out of prison for only two weeks. The man had received Jesus into his life while in prison. Now that he was reunited with his family, who were not Christians, they were all struggling in their relationships. Unbeknownst to the father and the person talking to him, two other people got "the nudge" from God for the children and the mother. After about an hour of ministry, the mother and their teens in separate conversations gave their lives to Jesus, and the father had been encouraged to keep pressing on. Heaven was having a blowout party that night as this family was united spiritually, as well as physically.

At this point, I think I need to share a little strategy for how I witness personally. I've been sharing my faith with people on the street since 1981. Non-Christians have stereotype images of who we are and what they think we're all about. They think being a Christian is being very religious and looking like you are baptized in lemon juice. So, I try to dispel that image within the first minute, so I can get them to stay in the conversation. I may make some opening remarks that may lead them to assume that I may be a Christian. My response will be almost automatic, "Yes, I am." Then I smile (very important) and say, "If you think what it is to be a Christian is what you do one or two hours a week on Sunday, you've missed the point by a country mile." Then I hold my hands up about a foot or so apart and say, "This is a week... 168 hours end to end." Then I take my thumb and forefinger and hold them about an eighth of an inch apart and say, "This is church! It's not about this! It's about this!" and I go back to a foot apart. "But church is where you learn how to do this successfully. We all have needed someone to teach us how life was designed to work and taught by someone who knows more about the "owner's manual" than we do. Ninety percent of the Bible teaches us how to do life. Look around; there are a lot of people who don't know how to do life." To the unsaved, this is a revelation, and that makes my approach a little different and interesting.

I have seen a lot of Christians witness, and I've learned a lot of what gets good results and what gets bad results. A little small talk goes a long way when it comes to sharing your faith with a stranger. Anything, even the weather, can be the icebreaker that allows you to start talking and showing yourself friendly. It has been said that the difference between a stranger and an acquaintance is, "Hello, my name is..."

If this is a one-time meeting and you may never see each other again, then you may look for an opportunity to turn the conversation toward spiritual things rather quickly. But if this is a friend, co-worker, or relative, then the strategy would be a little different, which we will talk about later in the book.

After you have turned the conversation toward spiritual things, you might say, "I'm sure you know who Jesus is, by reputation, but have you ever met Him?"

This is a question that is almost guaranteed to get a response. "Meet Him? Oh, right. Now you're going to tell me He stood right in front of you, and you shook His hand."

"No, I never said that. What if you were on the phone with the President of the United States for an hour and you both talked about many different personal things: Do you now have a relationship with him?

Does it really require a face to face meeting to have a relationship?"

People understand these kinds of relationships, especially with social media today, which now opens the door of their understanding even more. People meet online all the time now. They talk about their deepest desires, needs, hurts, and broken relationships before they ever have a face to face meeting.

"Prayer is kind of like a cell phone. No wires are attached, yet the person on the other side not only hears but can respond as well. But if we don't call, He won't answer."

I have also heard people in the world say if we talk to God, that's prayer. But if God talks to us, that's schizophrenia. (Just had to throw that one in.) But don't we know better? He can and wants to talk to us, just not in a way we are used to.

I quite often end everything I say with a question. Christians think that the best way to maintain control of the conversation is by how much they talk. **It's not. It's about asking the right questions** that will probe their minds to even think about this subject.

Asking questions about another person says that you are interested in them. Be quiet, and do not answer the question for them. And don't look away. Looking away says you are not really interested in what they have to say. Look them in the eyes. Remember, God gave you two ears and only one mouth. If you listen twice as much as you talk, especially early in the conversation, you'll get farther. If you ask a question and they don't respond, cock your head and give them the little puppy dog look. This indicates to them that you are waiting for an answer. If you still don't get a response, raise your eyebrows. Nothing is worse in a conversation than silence, and since you asked the question, the burden is on them.

One question I ask sometimes is: "Did you know that the ones in Heaven tonight are only there for one reason? Do you know what that reason is?"

If they respond with, "No." Your answer is, "Because they chose to be there. God won't force you, and neither can I. It's really up to you."

Often times in a conversation, people make comments concerning their insignificance as an individual or that they have done so much wrong God could not have any interest in them or forgive them. They make self-demeaning statements such as, "Out of all the billions of people in the world, why would God care what happens to me?" This is a perfect opportunity to enlighten them.

Hold up your index finger and explain to them, "You clearly missed this one important fact." With a surprised look, they usually ask, "And what's that?" This time you point to that index finger and explain. "You missed the fact that this fingerprint is one of a kind. Nobody in the world has this fingerprint, that's why law enforcement uses it for identification. After God made you, He broke the mold. He shaped and molded you in your mother's womb. He knows the number of hairs on your head (and in my case, the number that used to be there). He gifted you with your talents and abilities that set you apart from everyone else. He has also set a place for you at His dinner table, with a personal placard with your name on it. It's called the marriage supper of the Lamb. If you're not there, He'll know who was supposed to be in that seat, and you will be missed. You have to enter into this relationship voluntarily; it can't be forced." You can further explain the salvation message if you feel they need to hear it.

This explanation can be so significant in opening their eyes and understanding. Make sure you give them ample time to digest and respond to the picture you just painted.

At the start of this book, I said the number one fear is I don't know what to say or who to say it to. Once you have opened the conversation naturally, a simple question like, "So, were you raised in a church? What's your understanding of God? Or "Are you interested in spiritual things?" Upon their response, you will have helpful information to begin asking probing questions that will give you a foundation of their understanding of spiritual issues.

If the answer is yes, continue with, "Could I ask what kind of church you went to?" This response will be one of the most helpful in understanding their foundation. No matter what their answer is, don't act shocked, and most of all, don't laugh. "Ha-ha-ha. You believe what? Ha-ha-ha. You believe that trash, you're going to hell!" At this juncture, the conversation is over! You can't insult someone's beliefs and then expect them to listen to anything you have to say. You simply nod your head in the affirmative. It doesn't mean you agree with them; it's simply acknowledging that you are interested and listening.

The next question is pivotal. "Do you still go to church?"

If the answer is yes, your work *may* be over. But if the answer is, "No," then I'm going to continue to probe. "Would it be too personal for me to ask why you don't go anymore?"

There could be many reasons, let's consider a few. They have been offended by someone and put the blame on the church instead of holding the offending party responsible for their actions. Or they asked God for something that was really important to them like the life of a loved one, and they didn't get the answer they wanted. Or they could have gone to a church where they never saw a prayer answered, a miracle, or anything else that would lead them to believe that God is real and wants a personal relationship with them. But what I'm really trying to do is reach the core issues that are separating them from God, so that I might be able to bridge that gap. We need to always keep in mind that you want to be a bridge-builder and to get to the real heart issues. Ask the Holy Spirit, "What are you doing in this person's life? How can I cooperate with the work you have already begun?"

For example, I was at Mardi Gras in New Orleans and carrying a placard on a stick. This is the only time of the year I look the part of a Jesus freak, the sign is not even mine, I just borrow it. I was standing just off Bourbon Street taking a break from a long day of witnessing when a clean-cut looking gentleman of about thirty-five years of age walked up and stood in front of me. He crossed his arms over his chest and squared his shoulders back and, with an almost belligerent attitude, stated, "I'm agnostic and immovable!"

I knew he either didn't know the definition of the word "agnostic," or he was just getting ready to try and jerk me around. The term agnostic simply means; I don't know if there is a god. So, how could you be agnostic and immovable? I was tired and not really up to someone horsing around with me, but either way, I thought, *Let's give it a try and see what happens.* After all, he did take time to come over and stand in front of me, maybe he really does want to talk. So, I responded with, "OK, I'll bite, why?" He began to talk.

I let him talk for about ten minutes, but when I realized that he was going around the same mountain for the fourth time just using different words. I decided it was time to speak,

"Sir, I've been listening to you for quite a while now, and I've noticed something I don't think you see. All I've heard so far is that the pastor is a money-grubber, and everyone else in the church is a hypocrite. But I didn't hear you say anything bad about God. Your problem isn't with God; it's with man. Do you think that is accurate?" I stopped and waited for a response.

He contemplated my comments for a moment, eyes opened wide, grin on his face, and said, "Wow, that's true!"

As I continued, I don't know if this was a sheer guess or the leading from the Lord, but I said,

"I think I might know what happened. I could be wrong, so bear with me and see if any of this sounds familiar. I think somebody dragged you into a church when you didn't want to be there. Tried to jam Jesus down your throat when you weren't ready to receive Him, and they weren't going to let you out of there until they got some response from you that satisfied them. So, you not only took offense at them but at the pastor and the whole church thing. But not at God, or you wouldn't be here talking with me."

I stopped talking and let him ponder what I had just said. It's important for Christians to know when to be quiet and let people think. This is when they are digesting things you say, and if you don't let them think, they can't properly respond to your explanations.

He looked at the ground for about two whole minutes before he looked at me and said, "You are absolutely right."

I replied, "Now, you only have two questions facing you. But first, forget church. Church isn't the issue."

He already had a bad taste in his mouth concerning church, so I took it off the table. Then I continued,

"The first question you have to ask yourself is this: 'Is God real?' If the answer is yes, then secondly, what should your relationship with Him look like? Everything else will work its self out."

"Man, that makes sense," he responded with a big smile.

He thanked me and disappeared around the corner, and I immediately began to pray for him. Seconds later, he came back and took my wrist with one hand and shook my hand with the other, and said again,

"Thank you. You don't have any idea how much you just helped me."

"You're welcome, glad I could help." Then he again shook my hand.

You see, first I listened, then I spoke right to the point concerning his issues. "Forget church? Are you crazy?" you might be thinking. If he gets right with God, he'll end up in church, anyway. I was just removing a temporary obstacle between him and God.

We had a sixteen-year-old that went through our Hollywood Mission Trip a few years ago. He had never witnessed before, and his method was to walk up to someone on the street and simply introduce himself, "Hi, my name is Jeremy. I've come all the way across the country just to talk with you about Jesus. Do you know Him? Do you have any relationship with Him?" It's key to mention here that he walked up slowly and calmly to people, not scaring them. He spoke clearly and distinctly, he listened to them, and by the end of the week, he had led six people to the Lord and had many powerful conversations. Now, if you choose to do it this way, a couple of things you want to remember.

1. Speak in a soft, natural voice.
2. Speak slowly.
3. Don't act nervous.
4. Shake their hand and smile.
5. Look them in the eye, but don't be weird about it.
6. Be polite and authentic.

If you are nervous, you will make them nervous. If you are a man, you will especially make a woman nervous. They won't hear what you have to say; they will only be thinking, *What's this person doing? What does he really want?* You need to put them at ease with your casual but sincere attitude.

If you are doing any kind of street evangelism, it's important to work in teams of two or three whenever possible. One male and one female helps to put the recipient at ease.

CHAPTER 7

The Content of Conversations— Share Your Story

Over the years of teaching evangelism, I have been amazed to find how many people thought there was only one way to preach the gospel to someone, and that was straight forward and to the point. Or they felt they needed to sound like their pastor on Sunday morning to be effective. Your pastor has a different relationship with his congregation than he does with the unsaved. He might close his message with, "Every head bowed and every eye closed," giving an opportunity for people to respond to an altar call. That is totally different than you would do if you are talking to an individual.

To "preach" the gospel simply means conveying the good news that Jesus put on skin and took an "earth walk" for thirty-three years to show us what God, the Father, was like. He died on a cross for our sins and was raised from the dead three days later, and then ascended to Heaven so that the Holy Spirit could now come and live in any of us who choose to invite Him into our lives.

We most often think that every conversation has to contain Scripture to be considered witnessing or to be effective. This isn't true. I may start on what could be considered common ground and later introduce scriptures to make points as to what God says about the subject. If I can't gain their confidence early, I won't be able to hold them long enough to get into the meat of the Word.

I also meet people who don't want to receive what I have to say; they just want to argue. In these situations, I turn up the heat to help them better understand the seriousness of this subject. Let me give you some examples.

I was talking with a guy who just didn't want to hear about Jesus. I sensed this conversation was going to end soon, so I decided to take a chance by shocking him.

So, I said, "So I guess you just want to go to hell and be with your friends."

He literally jumped a half step back and said, "I didn't say I wanted to go to hell."

So, then I said, "Well, it's clear to me that you really don't understand the things of God, but you don't want to talk to anyone like me. Listen, man, you can't make an intelligent decision on a subject of this importance, literally a matter of life and death, on hearsay, myth, or popular opinion. You give me a few minutes, and I'll give you the facts. What you do with that information is your business; it's between you and the Big Guy."

And he stood there and listened. Why? In this case, I made it clear he needed facts. And two, because it had to be his decision. Which translates into "No pressure". But did he pray with me? No. This was the first time he ever heard the things I told him. He needed time to digest all this valuable information. Let me assure you, if he doesn't accept Jesus's invitation, he will never stand before God and say he didn't understand!

While witnessing at the Gay Pride Festival in West Hollywood, a lesbian, maybe in her mid-twenties, came up to me with her bubbly personality and a clipboard with a petition about some kind of legislation having to do with abortion. She was trying to get people to sign to push this vote through. (I believe it had to do with the partial-birth abortion issue, and I wondered why a lesbian would be concerned with abortion anyway.)

I became contemplative for a moment and then replied, "I'm sorry, but I really can't sign that."

Still bubbling, she asked, "Well, why?"

"Because about a month ago, I was watching the news and they were telling a story of a little girl who was celebrating her second birthday. They were showing a video of this little girl running around with some other children, giggling and playing. They reported that she was physically, mentally, and emotionally normal. And the reason that was newsworthy was that when this girl was born, she weighed less than one pound."

I held out my hand, palm up, cupped, and pointing to my palm as if she was in my hand. I continued, "You could have held her in the palm of one hand. I've eaten steaks bigger than that! And she lived outside her mother's womb. And you want me to sign something that says it's OK to kill her?" Then more softly, I said, "I can't do that."

Her effervescence evaporated before my eyes. Her clipboard went under her arm, and she turned and walked away slowly while staring at the ground. I never quoted a verse of scripture or even mentioned the name of Jesus, but I still witnessed to her. I might have been able to pursue the conversation, but I think she needed time to digest what I had just told her. I not only just proved to her why abortion is wrong, but that the Creator is right. The further implication would be, if God is right about this, what else could He be right about?

Another example is one that I heard on the radio. It was on Focus on the Family. James Dobson was playing a tape of a man that was sharing, I think, in a church somewhere. I had tuned in late, so I didn't hear who he was or where he was speaking.

The man speaking on the radio was a national speaker. He was on a plane one day when he engaged in conversation with the man next to him. He asked the man what he did for a living, and they talked about that for fifteen minutes when this man reciprocated. The radio speaker informed him that he spoke in conferences and conventions on three subjects, one of which was abortion. About then, a man in the row in front of them heard this and turned around and said he was pro-choice. The Christian speaker simply asked him a series of questions concerning his stand and dispelled each of them with compelling arguments and never once quoted a verse of scripture. At the end, the man responded with, "You're the first Christian that ever made any sense. Every time I disagree with a pro-lifer, all they do is quote scripture. After talking with you, I'll have to go home and reevaluate my stand."

I think right here would be the best place to explain a strategy I use when talking with people. You'll have to use your imagination because I usually do this live. Imagine me holding a very dry sponge in my left hand—one that's about six inches wide by eight inches long and about one and a half inches thick. And in the other hand is a glass of water. Now I know the sponge will hold all the water in the glass, but if I just dump this glass of water on this sponge, where will most of the water end up? That's right, on the floor. Why? Because the sponge is too dry to absorb all that water so quickly.

The sponge represents unsaved people who are very spiritually dry. Who are you? You are the glass of water. In some cases, a Fire Hydrant! A sip from a fire hydrant could blow them into the next block. By definition, that would be trying to tell them everything you ever learned in Sunday School until today in one conversation. Don't do that.

It would be better to just give them a sip and gently massage it into the sponge, which would be like one of your great stories of what God has done in your life, like the 2-1-1 technique. You talk about it, they ask you questions about your story, you answer their questions. When you turn the sponge over, the water stays where it's supposed to stay. Then someone else comes along and gives them another sip, but it will take less massaging to get it into the sponge because there is moisture already there.

In other words, it will be easier to give the sponge only what it's able to absorb at one time. It would be better to leave the sponge a little thirsty and desiring more than to flood them, and they reject you and the message.

Take the word "Preach" and take the letter "P" off, what are you left with? That's right, "Reach." There's nothing more important than reaching somebody with an explanation that makes sense to them. We need to make this so super simple that nobody can say they didn't get it, or it didn't make sense.

Our brain is a super complex computer. When we were born, we were all equipped with this basic operating system. Everything else is programmed into it by life experiences or teaching. Also, computer programmers teach us, you will only get out what you have programmed in. If you program your mind with King James English, that is what will come out. This may be a revelation for some, but Jesus didn't speak sixteenth century Elizabethan English, he spoke in the language of His time. Shouldn't we? If we quote a scripture to someone and it comes out in King James, it might as well have been Greek or Hebrew, they don't understand that either. I recommend that you do your primary reading and study out of more modern versions to prevent this. I use New King James as my regular study and preaching Bible, but on my computer, I always still have all the modern versions as well to get a well-rounded understanding.

We also need to lose our "Christianese". To the unsaved, terms as simple as "fellowshiping," could mean four guys in a rowboat with fishing poles and a six-pack. We may use the word repent, but their minds will conjure up a cartoon with a guy wearing sandwich signs reading "Repent, the world ends tomorrow!" You say "devil," they see the guy in the red flannel suit with a pitchfork.

It would also be good to leave your $12.50 words at home. I find that most Christians can't give me an accurate definition of "Jesus was the propitiation for their sins," but they'll use it on the unsaved. Use simple words that can be understood. We must be clear because their lives hang in the balance.

Now take the word "Reach" and take the letter "R" off and you are left with "Each," each one according to their ability to understand. Be all things to all men that you may win some.[8]

I learned most of what I know about computers from Walter Haack. He took care of maintenance and repairs for all our office computers a number of years ago. At that time, even though he didn't have a relationship with God, he was so impressed with the work we were doing in Hollywood with the youth, that he wouldn't charge us for labor, only parts. I began sharing with him a little here and a little there about God.

One day he called and said, "I'm getting ready to go into the hospital for an operation, and I would like you to pray for me before I go in." I smiled on the other side of the phone because I knew it was time to sit him down and spell out the salvation message in no uncertain terms. I had a problem with one of our computers,

_____

8 1 Corinthians 9:22

so it was easy to get him to come to the Oasis, so I could pray for him.

When he was done fixing the computer, I brought him into my office and said, "Walter, we need to talk. You know that I have not always had a relationship with God. I was thirty-one years old when I discovered that I could have a personal relationship with the Living Creator and have my sins forgiven. You could have that kind of relationship with the Lord and an assurance that you will go to Heaven when you die."

After some discussion, I made the offer for him to receive Jesus as his personal Lord and Savior. His response was emphatic, "Absolutely, I want that." I then told him how to go about praying, or I could lead him in a prayer.

"No, I would like to do it myself." was his reply. He began with, "Lord, it's been a l-o-n-n-n-g time since I talked to you last." He prayed for a couple more minutes and then stopped. I looked up to see what he was doing. His head was still down, but he was looking left, then right, and then said, "Amen." He wanted to make sure that he had covered all the bases.

Walter once told me, "I can't believe how God or anyone could keep track of every person in the whole world at one time. It's impossible." Then he said the same day, "I was trying to contemplate the contents of a 520MB hard drive. This means it's half a gigabyte, and the average computer being sold today has over 500 gigs hard drive as standard equipment. This means 520,000,000 bytes of information are contained on this one hard drive. A byte is the space eight characters occupy. So, that is 520 million bytes times 8 equals the number of characters on this drive. Then it struck me. If man could build this, what could God do? Then I knew God was online." He smiled and commented, "I knew God was real, and I was ready to give my heart to the Lord months before. Remember the night we were working late on one of your 'stubborn' computers, and you shared with me the story of how you got saved or your 'revelation of God,' I was ready that night." (*Your Story Matters*)

I never saw any indication that he was ready, so I decided to wait for another opportunity before asking him. The next day Judy, my wife, and I picked up some flowers and went to the hospital to visit Walter after the operation. We walked into the room, gave Walter a hug, and he introduced us to his friend standing on the other side of the bed. We commented, "We've been praying for you all day." His friend smirked a little and popped off, "He needs a lot of prayers. Oh, yea, I can see God up there, saying, 'Walter? Walter, who?'"

Walter, lying in bed, looked up at her with an indignant look on his face and said, "Hey, watch it; my name is now on God's hard drive." Since then, Walter has become one of my very good friends.

Just as God communicated to Walter through his understanding of computers, He can use almost any analogy to help people grasp His message to them. Like I said before, it didn't all happen in one conversation, in church, or with a Bible in my hand.

Jesus used parables to get His points across. Parables are just analogies with spiritual meanings behind them. He talked about sheep, shepherds, vines, and vineyards because those things were common among the people of His day. I was in preaching in a church in Texas and was trying to make this point and said, "Let's be realistic here; how many of you have sheep in your backyards?" I laughed when six hands went up, "OK, OK, maybe that is true here in this part of the country, but that's not true in most of our cities. You get the point!" It's important that we find analogies that people of today can relate to.

Let me give you one such analogy that I frequently use because it relates to almost anyone in our society. After you have started a conversation with one or more people, be sure to ask their first name. Asking for only their first name could dispel any fear that you are going to find them on the internet and harass them by phone or social media. Then I say, *"You know, it's ok to date God, don't you?"* If this person is by himself or herself, you are going to give them a hypothetical boyfriend or girl-friend. If the person you are dealing with is female, de-scribe to her an attractive male. Paint a picture in her mind.

Let's say you have a boyfriend and his name is Sean. He's six feet tall with dark hair and blond streaks. He's rather buff, but not overly done. He's got a six-pack, un-like my pony keg. (This is a good place to add a little hu-mor. It sets a relaxed atmosphere while still getting the point across on a very serious subject. Most Christians get very tense when they are sharing their faith)

Often times they have someone they are dating or maybe just started dating. They will become locked into this story just to find out what happens to their charac-ter. Let's pretend, You two have been dating for about six months now (and you could put in a nervous giggle here), and you come out of a movie, and you both get in the car. Before he starts the engine, he stops, turns, and looks into your baby blues and says,

"Babe, you are everything I ever dreamed about in a woman. You are all I think about. And as a token of my love for you, I've taken you to the 'chick flick' mov-ies, taken you out to candlelit, gourmet dinners, taken you to do outreach at the Oasis in California (planting a seed, to you the reader). I've come to the conclusion that you are the one I want to spend the rest of my life with. If you will marry me (time for the second giggle), this is what I will offer you. When I complete my education, I'm going to be an engineer. I'll make a good living, and we'll build a house in the suburbs with a white picket fence, and we'll have six kids... well, how about two, and live happily ever after. (Any time you deal with anything having to do with sex, you will always get a giggle here) What do you think?"

Now she's caught a little off guard. Her forehead scrunches as she bites her bottom lip, and she responds with something like this.

"Aw Sean, I know you love me, but I'm not ready to make this kind of a commitment right now."

He reaches out to take her hand and immediately responds with,

"That's alright, I understand. No pressure, I just had to let you know how I feel. Take your time. When you're ready, you let me know, and we'll get married, OK?"

"Well, he's cute, he makes me laugh, and he spends lots of money on me," she thinks.

So, she keeps dating him. I call this time the M&M syndrome. This is where you have to get past the candy coating on the outside and see if it's pure milk chocolate inside or just a nut.

If it's a guy you are talking to, you can say something like this to make him laugh.

"If you want to see what she's really like, wake her up at 8:00 a.m. on a Saturday morning, and that should give you a peek as to what she would be like twenty years from now."

"Well, another six months goes by, and you finally come to the conclusion that he's my hunk, and I can't live without him." (Another giggle) "So what do you do? Call your best friend and tell her to tell him that you accept his proposal."

"Heck, no! You get him back in that car, and you bat those long fake eyelashes at him, and you tell him you accept his proposal."

Now you bring it home using Scripture.

"This is how God views us. He said, 'I love you so much, and as a token of my love for you, I let my Son go to the cross for you, for your sins. If you will commit your life to me, this is what I will offer you—a new life on this earth and an eternal life with me in Heaven. Love, peace, joy, and forgiveness for all your sins can be yours every day no matter what your circumstances."

The most famous verse in the Bible is John 3:16 (NKJV), "For God so loved the world, that He gave his only begotten Son that whoever would believe in Him should never perish, but have ever lasting life." The word "believe" in this verse doesn't mean if I walk over to the light switch and flip it, I "believe" the light will come on. It's not just head knowledge. Amplified Bible interprets the word as "...believe in, rely on, trust in, put all your confidence in the Lord Jesus Christ, and you will be saved." What the word really means is to commit to Him, just like in a marriage commitment.

In the Bible, His people are referred to as the Bride of Christ. There are also many analogies in the Bible comparing our relationship with Him as a marriage, which is a total commitment.

I explain, "Jesus begins to paint a picture of what he's offering us. First thing, I save you from an eternal separation from Me, which is hell. This is what he offers for us on the earth. I'll give you an abundant life with peace and joy. I'll teach you how to be a husband to your wife and a father to your kids. I'll teach you how to be an employee to your employer or an employer to your employees. I'll teach you how to handle all your finances, and I'll watch over you all the days of your life and cause you to prosper. And when it's time for you to come home to Heaven to be with me, this is what I have for you."

"In Heaven, I have a specially prepared mansion for each of my children. There is no more sickness or disease, no more pain, no more tears, no more loneliness."

"And just as Sean can't force you to love him and you can't force him to love you, neither will God force you. The only people in heaven tonight are there for one reason; they chose to be there. It's your choice; nobody else can make this decision for you. You don't have to make this decision today, but just as with a boyfriend or girlfriend, you are going to have to bring this relationship to a conclusion, one way or another. He has already demonstrated how much He loves you, how will you respond?"

Let me assure you that any conversation that deals with the issues of God are all good. And once again, I say it doesn't all have to happen in one conversation. As a matter of fact, statistics show that the average Christian has been witnessed to six times before they got saved. So, where does that place the person you are talking to: one, three, five, or seven? The circumstance frequently sets the stage for how the conversation should go.

Don't think you failed if they don't pray with you. We're seed planters. We don't always get to see the harvest, but that's ok since we're planting God's incorruptible seed. We just have to remain positive and know He is more than able to tend to His seeds. Another opportunity may arise in the form of what I call the Third Person Technique. Many years ago, I was a building contractor and did a lot of home remodels. I often wore a Christian t-shirt that had some little catchy phrase on it that would let the world know where I stood on things. People hired me to remodel their homes, not to preach to them. There were many times that they would either inquire of me what the shirt meant or what I did for fun. I replied, "On weekends, I often go out on the streets and see who I can find that needs help from Jesus." That kind of answer stirs more questions. "You mean you actually walk the street and just stop people and try to talk to them about religion?"

"Well, yes. But let me explain." At this juncture, you can steer the conversation in any direction. What I would often do is tell what I say and how someone might respond, then what I would say next and why. By the time I was done telling them what I did and how I did it, I have shared Jesus with them. Everything except an altar call. So, it didn't sound like I was trying to witness to them, but I get all the major points across.

Another Third Person Technique, which I found works well, is taking advantage of the elevator awkward quietness. Did you ever notice that the more you whisper on an elevator, the more people strain to hear what you are saying? A friend and I would get on an elevator, and as soon as the door shuts, whether anyone else is talking or not, one of us would start whispering something like this,

"Have you ever heard of being born-again? Bill said that I had to become born-again if I wanted to go to heaven."

I asked, "What in the world does that mean?"

He replied, "I just needed to tell God I'm sorry for all that I've done wrong in the past, including ignoring

Him, and then invite Him into my heart and life, and that's all it takes."

My friend would respond with, "He's right. I did that many years ago, and my life has never been the same. I wouldn't hesitate if I were you."

This exchange took about thirty seconds, as long as it took to get to your floor. The door opens, you get out, but you leave life-changing information, a "divine seed" behind.

While in any conversation, consider telling them how you came to Christ. Why? Because *Your Story Matters!*

CHAPTER 8

Equipping the Saints

One night our family was sitting around the dinner table. And we were discussing personalities, talents, and temperaments, and it was at this point that I committed the cardinal sin. Turning to our thirteen-year-old daughter, I smiled and declared,

"You know Melissa, you're just like your mother."

At first, her response was not so good.

I said, "Wait a minute, you misunderstand, let me explain." Then I began to describe her as I saw her.

"Melissa, I see that you are very intelligent, organized, analytical, and very much a planner. I see that you are very determined to accomplish your plans. You are willing to work hard and to pay the price for the goals that you have set for yourself. Yet you have remained compassionate and loyal to your family and friends. You're nurturing and caring."

She sat there looking at me with her jaw hanging and staring like a deer in headlights.

When I was finished, all she could say was, "Wow, thanks."

"No thanks are necessary. I'm not giving you anything; I'm just stating what I see in you."

Of course, I was only stating her positive traits!

Why was she so surprised? Couldn't she see these traits in herself? I don't think so, and here is why. Since this is how she always has been, how she has always thought, responded, and handled herself, she has no other "Her" inside to compare herself with. You can look at someone and try to evaluate that individual, but unless you can be on their inside, you'll never know exactly how they think and why. It takes a good teacher, mentor, or coach who can look at someone, see their strengths, and help them refine them into something that will be profitable for their lives. As well as deal with the weaknesses that can keep a person from being all that they were designed to be.

Let me give you another example. What about a professional baseball player? How do you think his career began? Let's try a hypothetical situation.

Every father loves to have a son to do guy stuff with. So, let's say his son's name is Mark and it's his seventh birthday. His father buys him a baseball bat, ball, and glove. Throwing the ball up in the air, the father enthusiastically hollers, "Come on, Son, let's go outside and play ball."

Mark replies with a discouraged voice, "Aw, Dad, I can't do that."

The father tries again, "Sure you can, Son, just give it a try."

"Daaaaad, I tried this before, and I can't do this."

The persistent father gets Mark outside, gives him the bat, and says,

"OK, Mark, I'll toss you the ball, and you hit it."

The father throws the ball, and Mark swings wildly, causing him to spin in a complete circle.

His face turns red with embarrassment, and Mark defends his stand, "See, Dad, I told you I can't do this."

The father grabs the bat and instructs, "Mark, stand with your feet this far apart. Hold the bat like this. Keep your eye on the ball. Come on, let's try it again."

This time the father throws the ball, and Mark hits a long one. "Wow! Dad, did you see that?"

"Yea, Son, I did. Now I have to go and get it."

So, the father throws the ball again. Mark hits it. Now he is really excited. Again and again, Mark hits the ball. Panting and rubbing his elbow, the father says, "That's enough for one day. I can't take any more." A potential career is launched.

Next, perhaps, he joins little league and is taught more about how to play the game. Then he plays high school ball, and maybe even receives a college scholarship. Then one day, a pro scout sees him play, and he is drafted into the majors. But you don't get to see him on television. No, first, he is off to the farm league, to be coached more. Each time there are coaches that see potential in this guy. They are less interested in where he is today. They are more interested in who he could be with the right coaching and personal commitment to training and practice.

I believe God looks at us the same way. He is less interested in who we are today; He is more interested in who we could be with Him in our lives. This is how we need to look at people in the world. We might not say it, but in our mind, think... *That old cigarette sucking sinner, you know, that old alcoholic, wife beatin' piece of trash down the road.* We need to look at them as God does. Think about how they could be with Him in their lives? Romans 5:8 describes God's feelings towards the lost, "He loved us so much, that while we were yet sinners, He died for us."[9] He sees who we could be if we would only let him do a work in us.

He knows our potential if we would only step out in faith and do what He called us to do... be a witness to the world. He gave the Church apostles, prophets, pastors, teachers, and evangelists as coaches in the game of Life to equip the body for the work of ministry (Ephe-

9 Paraphrased.

sians 4:11–12). Every position in the five-fold ministry has a two-part job. If you are a pastor, your number one job is to pastor the flock God has given you to watch over. Part two of your job is to raise up other pastors... an associate pastor, youth pastor, children's pastor, etc. You need to pour out your best into each one as they have need of your knowledge and experience, and most importantly, impart vision to reach people who desperately need to hear the Good News of God's love.

Not all are to be pastors or teachers, prophets, or apostles, but all are called to win souls or to do the work of an evangelist as we are told in 2 Timothy 4:5. I'm here to tell you, you can do it. You are called to do it, and if called, then anointed. I want to encourage you to be sensitive in your everyday life with people God puts around you for His Divine purposes.

There is a lot to be said about the Great Commission, I won't dwell on it long, but I can't assume everyone understands it either. Matthew 28:19–20 (NKJV) is the scripture that is quoted as the Great Commission.

*Go therefore and make disciples of all nations,
baptizing them in the name of the Father, the Son,
and the Holy Spirit, and teaching them to observe
all things that I have commanded you...*

However, I believe Jesus commissioned us when he spoke in John 20:21 (NLT), "As the Father sent Me, so I send You." Obviously, going to the cross was Jesus' job alone to do, but He has a job for each of us while we are on planet Earth.

In John 16:7–8 (ESV), Jesus is quoted as saying,

> *Nevertheless I tell you the truth, it is to your advantage that I go away; for if I don't go away, the Helper will not come to you; but if I depart, I will send Him to you. And when He has come He will convict the world of sin...of sin, because they don't believe in Me.*

The Helper *is* the gift of God for evangelism. We are workers together with Him to reach the lost (2 Corinthians 6:1). We can't do it without Him, and He has chosen to reach the world through us, His children. What an awesome opportunity, challenge, and privilege!

2 Corinthians 5:18 (NKJV) reads,

> *Now all things are of God, who has reconciled us to Himself through Jesus Christ, and has given us the ministry of reconciliation.*

I believe the key word in this verse is the word "through".

The Father was working *through* Jesus. This is why He came to Earth. Give me another reason why Jesus came to this Earth, other than reconciling man back to God. I want to know what it is. Everything else—healing, abundant life, destroying the works of the devil— these are all fringe benefits of having the Son of God on earth. Now, look how this plays out in 2 Corinthians 5:20 (and let's make this personal),

Now then, *you* are ambassadors for Christ, as though God were pleading through us; we implore you on Christ's behalf, be reconciled to God.

An ambassador is the highest legal representative of any king, kingdom, or nation to another nation. Who better represents God, but one who has first-hand knowledge of His goodness and has tasted what He is offering? Now that Jesus sits at the Father's right hand, we are now His ambassadors on this earth. We can speak with authority because the same Spirit that lived in Jesus, the Holy Spirit, lives in us.

In John 14:12 (NKJV), Jesus is speaking,

> *"Most assuredly, I say to you, he who believes in Me, the works that I do he will do also; and greater works than these he will do, because I go to My Father"*

What do you think of when you hear of the works of the Lord? Miracles? Healing the sick? Raising the dead? Have you tried to raise the dead lately? No? How about the spiritually dead? There are many people who are the "Walking Dead" and who need to know there is a power that can give them a new life. They can become a new creation. We, as humans, often focus on the miracles that Jesus did as the goal of ministry for ourselves and lose sight of what Jesus came here to do. Obviously, none of us are going to the cross. And I'm not saying that miracles can't or shouldn't be part of our ministries, I'm just saying they aren't the main focus of what we have been sent here to do. If you have compassion and are broken-hearted for the lost, you'll see the miracle-working power of God. The Bible describes Jesus as "going about doing good and then healing the sick." We need to go about doing good deeds every day through kind acts, loving words, and just bringing joy to others. Then look for those opportunities to pray for the sick in body, soul, or spirit.

For many years we have done what we call The Hollywood Mission Trip, where groups come to make week long mission trips with our ministry in Hollywood. For the last several years, we have had the teams take time to pray before we go on our outreaches and then be quiet and listen to see if the Lord gives a vision, impression, or speak something about who we should look for to minister to. One year, we had a Korean and Japanese Evangelical team who prayed before they went out. One person saw an American flag sewn onto other materials. As the teams walked down Hollywood Boulevard, they are sensitive to the impressions God has put on a few of the student's hearts, but they don't wait for only those things to appear. The one who saw the flag sewn onto material was particularly looking for this. He saw someone wearing a t-shirt with an American flag and thought maybe that's the person. Their team got into a conversation with this man wearing the t-shirt. They found out that he was a Vet and had killed thirteen people in three different wars that he had served in. One particular image stood out in his mind of a six or seven-year-old boy running towards his trench with a bomb strapped to him, and the Vet had to shoot him. Even though all the killings were done during different wars, this man was suffering from Post-Traumatic Stress Disorder (PTSD) and had become an alcoholic and homeless.

The group assured him that God's forgiveness was available to him and that God would help him to forgive himself. After about an hour and a half conversation, the sun had gone down and California nights generally drop quite a bit in temperature, the Vet pulled his jacket out of his backpack. The small group of young people talking to him all began to chuckle and whisper among themselves. His jacket had an American flag sewn on to it. The teenager who saw this during prayer was grinning from ear to ear and shared with him, "God showed me this morning during prayer an American flag sewn onto some other material. So, we know for sure that this encounter was divinely orchestrated."

They prayed with him to receive Christ and to be delivered from alcohol.

He shared, "Two weeks ago, I had a bus ticket and was ready to go home to Portland, Oregon, to check myself into a detox center, but I chickened out."

Stunned, they got big grins on their face and shared with him,

"We are from Vancouver, Washington, right across the river from Portland, and we will be leaving in a couple of days and can meet you there."

The next morning the team was having prayer time, Bible reading, and getting their marching orders for the day from the Lord. Three of the young men, all separate from one another, went to the leader and said, "We need to go find that man, and I feel like it's urgent to do it right now." The leader agreed to go search for him with the students. They found him on Hollywood Boulevard and began to beg,

"Hey man, we feel like God is telling us to help you get on a bus today and go to Portland and check in to the detox center. We'll go with you and cash in your old bus ticket and help you buy a new one."

They walked around the corner to the bus station, got a new ticket for the bus to Portland, which was leaving in just a few minutes. He was getting ready to get on the bus when the bus driver stopped him. "You can't get on my bus. I smell alcohol."

The leader of the group just so happened to be Korean, and he guessed that the driver might also be. He began to speak to him in Korean, so he wouldn't embarrass the newly converted man.

"Sir, do you believe in second chances? Do you believe God can transform someone?"

"Yes, I do. I'm a Christian."

"Good! This man's second chance is in your hands."

Then the youth leader explained the story to him and what their plan was. The next day they got a call from the Vet, saying that he had arrived and checked into the detox center.

A man's life was transformed because a courageous teenager decided to do spiritual warfare and listened for God's marching orders. Then went out to obey the orders.

Another verse that really demonstrates what I'm saying here is Luke 4:18 (NKJV), where Jesus is speaking and quotes Isaiah 61:1 that spells out what He was supposed to do:

> *"The Spirit of the Lord is upon Me, because He has anointed Me to preach the gospel to the poor; He has sent Me to heal the brokenhearted, to proclaim liberty to the captives and recovery of sight to the blind, to set at liberty those who are oppressed; to proclaim the acceptable year of the Lord."*

He said today this is fulfilled in your hearing. Now, re-read this verse and put your name in it, and you'll see God's purpose for your life.

But if this wasn't exciting enough, look at John 15:16 (NKJV).

> *You did not choose Me, but I chose you and appointed you that you should go and bear fruit and that your fruit would remain...*

I am not a theologian, but I was curious about the word "appointed," so I looked in other versions of the Bible, such as; New King James, New International Version, New American Standard, Amplified, and one or two others. They all used the same word. But then I went to the King James Version the word used there was "ordained".

My wife and I have staff, and we can appoint one of them to take out the trash, and any of them could do that. We also have a youth pastor. We could appoint him to that position, but we can't anoint him to do the job, only God can anoint him. When you read not only this verse, but these three chapters John 14, 15, and 16, you see that He's talking about kingdom work.

> *"You did not choose Me, but I chose you and*
> *have ordained you, that you should go and bring*
> *forth fruit, and that your fruit should remain..."*
>
> (John 15:16 KJV)

You are gifted by God with the same Spirit Jesus had to share with the lost, and He will bring conviction of sin in the hearts of those who need what He has to offer—salvation.

In John 15:11 (ESV), Jesus says,

> *These things I have spoken to you that My joy*
> *may remain in you and that your joy may be full.*

The apostle Paul said about Jesus,

> *...For the joy set before Him, He endured the*
> *cross...*
>
> (Hebrews 12:11 NIV)

This was not only the joy of providing salvation for all those who lived in His day, but for all those that would follow. That joy comes to us on the installment plan, one soul at a time. What a thrill it is to know that God would use someone like me to help carry out His plans.

Anyone who has ever led another person to Christ knows this joy he's speaking of here. But I have to warn you, this joy He speaks about is addicting. You will lead one person to the Lord, and that will cause you to want to do it again and again. The more you do it, the more you will want to do it. Then one day, you will hit a slump, where you won't lead anyone to the Lord or even be able to engage someone in conversation. You will cry out to Him, "Why aren't you using me? What have I done wrong that you have removed your spirit from me?" Then you will remember reading this and realize you are going through withdrawal symptoms and that you really are addicted.

In the latter part of John 15:16 (KJV), it reads,

>...and whatsoever you ask the Father in my name, he may give it you.

This is the fourth out of six times in these three chapters, John 14, 15, and 16, where He says, "anything you ask the Father for, He will give it to you." Are we hard of hearing that we didn't hear Him the first time? Or is He trying to make a point. When you read these verses in context, you discover that the application of these verses deal more with ministering to people than personal consumption. If He called you to reach the lost, what do you need to accomplish the task?

As an example, in our ministry at Oasis of Hollywood, we have three shuttle buses, a mini-van, and a pick-up truck to meet our present transportation and ministry needs. We have prayed specifically for everything we have needed, and God not only gave it to us, but not one dime of it came out of our budget. Equally interesting was the replacement of one of our vans a number of years ago. In January at one of our staff retreats, we were praying over ministry needs when I prayed for a new or late model Ford fifteen passenger van with the new V-10 engine, power steering, power brakes, automatic transmission, air conditioning, and a tape deck. (The tape deck will let you know it was quite a few years ago.) Three weeks later, I remembered that I didn't specify the color, so I said, "Oh, by the way, Lord, could you make it silver, so it goes with the color scheme of the Oasis and wouldn't be a solar panel on wheels?"

In April, enough money came in to start the hunt for this van. I called a friend of ours who owns a Ford dealership and told him what we wanted, and he said he would start looking. Two weeks later, he called and said he had our van.

"Let me get the used car manager on the phone to describe it for you."

He said, "It's a three-year-old, fifteen passenger van with the new V-10 engine with only 31,000 miles on it. It has power steering, power brakes, automatic transmission, air conditioning, and a tape deck."

Now doesn't the Lord say He will give us above and beyond all that we can hope or believe for? He went on to say.

"It also has power windows and door locks, power driver's seat, and alloy rims."

I responded with, "Wow, it sounds like everything we are looking for, how much are we talking about?"

The price was less than I expected, so I told him we would come in the next day to see it. And before I could hang up he said, "Oh, by the way, it's silver!" Not only did we take the van, but we raised the balance of the money in two days. Enough to not only pay for the van but also to have Oasis of Hollywood letters put on it, as well.

If God will give us all the tools we need, such as buses and vans, buildings, and sound equipment, how much more will He give us the anointing we need to reach the lost? How much more boldness will He give you to overcome your shyness or put the words on your lips at the time you need it? He promised Moses, "Go Moses, I'll put the words in your mouth when you get there." Moses gave God sixteen reasons why he couldn't do what God wanted him to do. "B-B-B-But, God, I'm not eloquent. I stutter," Moses argued. When he obeyed God, he became effective at what God wanted him to do? My Bible says Pharaoh was ready to throw in the towel several times, but God wanted to really get glory and honor and to see that the children of Israel came out of Egypt with their hands full of gifts. What do you need to accomplish what God has called you to do? Boldness? Divine connection? Financial provision? Ask, and it *will* be given to you.

CHAPTER 9

Who Me? An Undercover Agent?

The Father equips us with what we need. Then calls and anoints us for a job. He sends us out into the world disguised as grocery clerks, construction workers, students, librarians, CEOs, and scientists. Kingdom Undercover Agents! Your talents have equipped you to hold down and flourish in all kinds of different jobs. And guess what? There are unsaved people all around you. You often even have jobs with paid vacations, medical, dental, and built-in retirement plans. Just so you can be a light and share the gospel thru your words and actions.

Don't take me wrong. We are supposed to give our employers eight hours of work for eight hours' pay. But you have before work, morning breaks, lunchtime, and afternoon breaks to reach your co-workers. I think nothing would be sweeter than sitting at a picnic table in your own backyard, sharing a platter of barbecued ribs with a co-worker that you have befriended. And when he asks you why you didn't lose your cool with the boss when he criticized you for something someone else had done. You respond with godly reasons. This is witnessing. As a matter of fact, the very way you responded now becomes a witness to your co-workers and can become a point of discussion.

Just befriending people you work with will eventually lead to an opportunity to share why you are the way you are. Sometimes, I think Christians can be too overbearing with their faith or just try to get it all done in one conversation. Often times, it would be better to wait and develop a relationship with co-workers before trying to share with them.

Do you know people that just rub you the wrong way? There are people you probably do your best to avoid just because they're just so raw, vulgar, and mean. The best thing you can do here is Colossians 3:12, 14 (NASB):[10]

> So, as those who have been chosen of God, holy and beloved, "PUT ON" (*because whatever you "put on" will be seen by those you encounter*) a heart of compassion, kindness, humility, gentleness, and patience...
>
> Beyond all these things, put on LOVE, which is the perfect bond of unity.

---

10 Italics are my words

From the very beginning, God created us to be just like him, Genesis 1:26 (NASB),

"Then God said; let Us make man in our image, according to our likeness; and let them rule..."

I like John 17:21 (NKJV), Jesus praying out loud, as one of the most profound things He has said:

That they all may be one as you Father are in Me, and I in you; that they also would be one in Us...

He doesn't mean we all should like baseball or Brussel sprouts. But, on the issues of life as God designed it, there would be no difference in our values or expectations. He told us to do everything He did and even greater things in John 14:12. Being the good parent that He is, He's not threatened by our doing great things. Nobody is going to take His place, no more than anyone could take your place.

Shoot, I wouldn't want His job! If I was packing His power, I would have fried a few people by now. I wanted to have our car fitted with laser cannons, but my wife wouldn't let me. I'm an Evangelist, and we live in Southern California. Our freeways live up to their reputation. Sometimes I'm guilty of saying out loud, *"You want to meet Jesus? Go ahead, sucker, cut me off again. I can arrange the meeting!"* (OK, I haven't arrived yet, He's still working on me.)

In John 15:15, Jesus says that He no longer calls us servants, but friends. I don't know about you, but my friends don't walk three paces behind me, nor me behind them. We walk side by side. Jesus is saying, come on, I told you everything the Father wants us to do, let's do this together. I'm not waiting for Him to do everything, but I'm going to do my job with the tools and anointing that He has made available to me. And I will bear fruit and fruit that remains because His word says so.

Have you ever read something many times, but then God changes the emphasis, and you see it in a whole different light? Well, that happened to me with this verse.

> *"But, if you love those who love you, what credit is that to you? Don't even sinners love those who love them?"*
>
> (Luke 6:32 NKJV)

The Lord revealed the latter part of that verse to me. If we would love them, they would love us! I don't mean warm fuzzy feelings, but getting serious about those people you absolutely can't stand. Why can't you stand them? Because they're not like you, and they have no relationship with Jesus, and they totally act like it, too. Those are the ones He wants to reach. The well don't need a physician!

The first step is to start to pray for them; I mean really pray for them. If you do, your attitude concerning them will change. You will find compassion welling up inside for them that will cause you to pray even more earnestly than you ever thought you could.

The second step is found in Romans 12:20 (NKJV),

> *If your enemy is hungry, feed him. If he's thirsty, give him a drink.*

Now I'm not talking about giving them a piece of dried sardine and a cup of water. Let's get a little more practical. You are on your way to work. It's near payday, the fridge is looking a little barren, so you slip through Mickie D's on your way to work and get a breakfast sandwich. Why not get two, and when you get to work, drop one off at the work station of that person who is hard to tolerate. Do not follow it with a three-point message. Just drop it and go to work. If they ask you why you gave it to them, you simply state, "I was hungry, and I thought you might be hungry." Now, this is not to happen every day or every week or even every month.

Maybe the next time, you both have had to work late the night before, and this morning you're "draggin' your wagon" trying to get to work, so you run through Starbucks, get one for them, too. No message to follow this act, either. When the time is right, they will start the conversation concerning your kindnesses. Don't get too spiritual with them; keep it light until they really warm up to you, you'll get your chance to share with them.

Back in the '80s, our focus was reaching teenage runaways. According to a police statistic, there were over 4,000 runaways on the streets of Hollywood on any given day. We ran the Oasis like a "supper club" on Friday and Saturday nights. Live bands and a hot meal was the bait we used to pack the place with standing room only on both nights. We never turned anyone away, so we didn't just attract runaways, but many homeless and local gangs. Judy, my wife, is a tender and compassionate woman. She would love on everybody equally. But she wouldn't take misbehavior from anyone for very long. Gang members would square off with each other quite regularly while in the Oasis. I can't tell you how many fights I had to break up. One night, one of these gangbangers started causing a ruckus, and it was starting to get serious. Judy went right over to him and told him to stop, sit down, and behave himself. He got two inches from her face with a tough smirk on his face and mouthed, "Or you'll do what?"

Just then, another gangster stood up between Judy and Mr. Tough Guy and made him back up and sit down. Why would he do that? Because even sinners will love those, who love them.

We have seen hard-core gang members come to the Lord this way through the Oasis. We just keep loving on them until their heart softens.

One of our spiritual sons is a guy we call Q. He was a tough dude from the gang called "The Crips". His best friend died in his arms from a drive-by shooting. But the love of God softened his hard heart, and he had a transformation in his life. He met his wife through our Hollywood Mission Trip (a good place to meet a future mate—mission field). Today, he and his wife have graduated from Christ for the Nations Bible College and Southwestern University. Where would he be today if we hadn't tried to reach him? Prison? The grave?

And think about it. Some of us get to wear some really cool outfits as undercover agents, like airline pilots or police officers. How about football players? Here's a true story, but I have omitted his name. One particular football player got to run out of the tunnel into stadiums full of cheering crowds. This guy had an ego bigger than the stadium, the world's biggest ego with feet. The quarterback would give him the ball, and he would score a touchdown. Then he would point to himself, "I'm the greatest! I'm the best! Me! Me!" Really irritating, don't you think? But then something happened. He gave his life to Christ, and everything changed. Then they gave him the ball, he scored, and then gave all the glory to God, the source of all his talent and ability.

Now realistically, what do you think the chances are of your getting close enough to someone like a pro-football player to share Jesus. Does it fall someplace between slim to none? So, if you can't get close to someone like him, who would have the best opportunity, another player perhaps? How about a coach? How about a coach like Joe Gibbs? He was the head coach of the Washington Redskins. He led them to three super bowl titles. Joe is a sold-out Christian and not ashamed to admit it.

Well, Joe Gibbs got out of football and involved himself in auto racing. He is the owner of multi-car teams. Today's NASCAR is not a bunch of back yard mechanics that scrape together a few bucks, build a car, and just run around in circles. It's big business. It takes millions of dollars just to campaign one car for a single season with millions at stake in prize money and lucrative corporate sponsorship. I met someone who knows Joe and says if you need to talk business with him, he'll take you in his office and talk business. But before you leave, he'll find out if you have a relationship with Jesus, and if you don't, he'll explain it to you. The reason is simple, he not only knows what he's paid to do, but he also knows what he's called to do. He knows if he takes care of God's business, God will take care of his business. As a matter of fact, he has won multiple championships in NASCAR's highest division.

The last figure I was aware of was that thirty-three out of the top forty-four drivers in the Cup Series are born-again Christians. This doesn't even include their crews. It's the only sport I know of that is so heavily saturated with Christians.

There are others that God has given high profile positions—like boxing. You wouldn't think that God would endorse a violent sport like this. However, many years ago, when Holyfield beat Tyson in their first fight (I didn't see the fight, but I did see the press conference following), Holyfield, on worldwide television, claimed he "served the only true God." Most people couldn't or wouldn't say that to another family member or co-worker, much less on national television. And why? Because he not only knows what he's paid to do, but he knows what he's called to do.

The point is this... God has gifted and placed His people in every facet of society so they can reach their sphere of influence. Where has He placed you? Have you ever tried to reach those around you? I can't reach your sphere of influence, nor can your pastor.

What will you do now? Will you step up to the plate and maybe feel foolish? Or will you hit some home runs for God and be one of His all-stars? What I showed you in the previous chapters is true, that you are not only called to do this job, but you are also anointed. And if so, how can you fail at this job? For you to fail, God would have to fail. The odds are pretty good that is not going to happen.

CHAPTER 10

Be a "Souldier" Doing Warfare

"Get off of the stage right now," I commanded the possessed man who was spitting out every foul expletive he could blurt out in between his demonic growls. As I explained earlier, in the early '80s, Friday nights at the Oasis were not typical church services by any means. We had live bands play, fed runaway teens, and ministered to them.

He came leaping off the stage, and it took five grown men to hold him down and bind the powers of darkness who were controlling this man. After his deliverance, the team ministered to him and shared with him that he needed to receive Jesus to be able to keep these evil forces from coming back and taking control of him. He refused to respond to the love of God by repenting and giving his life to the Lord. The next week he came back and was full of the devil and had to be picked up and carried outside by four guys.

Fortunately, not all spiritual warfare is so intense. Is there anyone in your life, friend or relative, which you have been praying for to come to know Christ, but you still haven't seen any changes in their life? Does it make you feel ineffective in prayer? Or do you just assume that they are hard-hearted? Do your prayers sound something like this? "Oh Lord, let your power fall on John Doe. Help him to come to know You as I know You. Let your mercy and grace be poured out on him and give him a taste of You and your goodness that he would give his heart to You."

That's not a bad prayer. But there is more that needs to be prayed. Scripture says that their (spiritual) eyes have been blinded by the god of this world (2 Corinthians 4:4). Could it be that they are being held back from moving towards God because they are in some form of bondage, and they just can't see and hear the truth.

Ephesians 6:12 (NKJV) says,

> *For we don't wrestle against flesh and blood, but against principalities, against powers, against and the rulers of the darkness of this age. I guess the bigger question should be, do you wrestle at all? We'll call on God to reach our loved ones and friends, but are we willing to do some spiritual warfare for them? We need to stand in the gap between them and the enemy of their souls and fight*

*for them because they don't know how or don't even
see their need?*

I'm not going to spend a lot of time on the subject of prayer. There are plenty of books written by those more knowledgeable than me. However, I would like to present some ideas that I feel directly affect evangelism in the area of spiritual warfare.

I was standing on a pier that protruded out into a lake when I began to see something very strange in a vision I had one time. I saw heads of people bobbing up and down all over the lake. The impression I had was that they were drowning in their sins. My eyes were drawn to one individual that appeared to be going down for the third time. I looked for something to throw to him, so he wouldn't drown. I found a life preserver with John 3:3 written on it and threw it out to him. He put his arm through the opening, and I felt satisfied he wouldn't go down now. Then all of a sudden, he and the life preserver disappeared below the surface. But once again, he came up coughing. I looked for something else to throw him and found another life preserver, and this one had John 3:16 written on it. I threw it out also, and he put his other arm through this one too. I felt assured that he couldn't possibly go down this time. Then suddenly, he and both life preservers were pulled below the surface. I called out, "What's going on, Lord?" He took me below the surface, and I saw a giant octopus on the bottom, and he had one of his tentacles wrapped around this guy's ankle.

I felt the Lord speaking to me, "No matter how many words you are throwing out to this guy, and even though he was receiving it, he couldn't do anything about it because he was in bondage. Draw the sword of the Spirit (Ephesians 6:17), which is My Word, and sever the tentacle that is holding this guy in bondage so that My word can do the job it was intended to do."

Matthew 16:18 says that the gates of hell will not prevail against us. The devil isn't trying to defeat us by running around and beating us over the head with a gate. Gates or doors were created to keep something in or something out. In this case, the devil is trying to keep the captives in and the saints of God out. With spiritual warfare, we kick in the gates of hell, bind the strongman, and set the captives free (Matthew 12:29). The battle for the souls of men and women are fought and won in our prayer time. Then we collect the spoils of our battles when we talk to people about Christ. I believe this is realized when you have been in warfare over someone, and then you get to talk to them and share about their need for Christ, and they say something like, "You know, that's the first time that ever made sense to me." This means your prayers have ripped off the blinders from their eyes, and they can see their need for Christ and the Lord's saving grace.

If your next question is, what verses do you use to combat the devil? Christian books on prayer will give you verses to use in your intercession. Over time and through your Bible studies, you will find many additional verses that can be used in warfare. When the devil came to tempt Jesus after He had been fasting in the wilderness, He responded to satan by quoting Scripture to him. The sword of the Spirit or the sword in the spirit world is God's Word. Jesus didn't just quote one verse, and satan fled, but He quoted specific verses dealing directly with each temptation before the tempter fled.

In Luke 10:19 (NKJV), it says

> *Behold, I give you the authority to trample on serpents and scorpions, and over all the power of the enemy, and nothing shall by any means hurt you.*

Let me break this down. The word *power* in this verse is two different words in the Greek. The first is *exousia*, which in this context actually means "authority".[11]

---

11 "Exousia Meaning in Bible - New Testament Greek Lexicon, Strongs Concordance - King James Version." 2020. Bible Study Tools. 2020. https://www.biblestudytools.com/lexicons/greek/kjv/exousia.html.

The second word for power in the Greek is *dunamis*.[12] In this context, it is used to describe the inherent ability or even miracle power. This is also the word where we get dynamite or dynamo. So, it might be translated to read; "Behold, I give you *authority* over all the *ability* of the enemy, and nothing shall by any means hurt you." But you must exercise the authority God has given you.

Think of it this way. You are in a room with no windows and only one door when a fire erupts between you and the door. The fire is spreading, and you are about to be overwhelmed with the smoke and heat. Suddenly, you discover a fire hose in the room. You pull the handle, and the water bursts out. Wala! The fire is extinguished. Who put the fire out, you or the water? If you answered the water, you're wrong. If you answered that you did, you are still wrong. You had to open the valve, or you would have burned to death. But only the water could quench the fire. Actually, it's a trick question. Both would be the correct answer. You had the authority to open the valve, but the water actually had the ability to put out the fire. You didn't have to beg the water to come out of the hose; it was under pressure, ready to go to work. *Our authority releases God's ability.* God has given us authority, but it's up to us whether or not we

---

12 "Dunamis Meaning in Bible - New Testament Greek Lexicon, Strongs Concordance - King James Version." 2020. Bible Study Tools. 2020. https://www.biblestudytools.com/lexicons/greek/kjv/dunamis.html.

use it. God's ability is released as we take the authority to defeat the enemy not only in our lives, but also in the lives of others. Sometimes the fire seems to be more of a forest fire, and it feels like we're trying to put it out with a garden hose. That is when we ask others to pray with us and get more hoses on the flames. Matthew 18:19 (NKJV) instructs us,

> *Again I say to you that if two of you agree on earth concerning anything that they ask, it will be done for them by My Father in heaven.*

Prayer is very important in doing Kingdom work. Jesus said, "Could you not pray with me for one hour? (Matthew 26:40). So many people think that is the allotted super-spiritual time that is needed to get answers. Sure, praying for one hour is good, but it isn't always necessary.

I think another way to pray is by agenda. If you have a need or you are just getting ready to share your faith on the streets, go into your "prayer closet" with an agenda and with all prayer and supplication with thanksgiving, let your requests be made known to God. Use your authority in the spirit realm, then get up and get out without looking at the clock.

The problem I see with this mentality is that many people, even leaders, specify we are going to pray for

X amount of time, maybe one hour. What if you have prayed and know that you are done, and it has only been forty minutes? Now, what are you going to do for the next twenty minutes... just look spiritual? Personally, I think this is one of the deterrents that keep us from praying more. If we would only pray what is required for that need to be met, we would be prone to pray for more things more often.

There have been many times that I have prayed for hours, but sometimes only a few minutes. I pray not just for those who I was going to be ministering to, but also for myself that He would help me be sensitive to the leading of the Spirit.

CHAPTER 11

Leaving Tracks
with Tracts

It was a cool evening in Southern California, with over 300,000 people leaving a major outdoor concert. My friend and I stood in the center of the exit gate, and I began to yell, "'High Times,' get your 'High Times' here, get them while they last." People fell into lines twenty to thirty deep just to get a little pamphlet. Just as fast as we could pass them out, people were taking them, and in a half-hour, every tract was gone. You might be wondering what is High Times. It was a drug user or doper's magazine. This tract or pamphlet had the Zig-Zag man (a symbol for a favorite brand of rolling papers for marijuana cigarettes) on the front and a marijuana leaf on the back, but the inside was a testimony of a drug user who met Jesus.

Ten years later, I was sharing this story in a class I was teaching when a guy came up to me and told me that he was about twenty people back when I ran out of tracts. He said he was backslidden at the time, but his friend, who had been vacillating on giving his life to Christ, got the tract, read it, and gave his life to the Lord. Some may say, "That was deceptive or even dishonest." But I disagree. It truly was a story of someone's "high times" and how they stayed eternally "high".

Tracts are, probably, the most underrated tools in the evangelists' arsenal. It can go to more places than you could ever go personally. They can go home with and talk to more people than you ever dreamed of. They can relate to the young and rebellious and the elderly facing their last days on earth. They can challenge the intellectual in ways that either stumps them or open avenues of new possibilities. They can tell the story of personalities from a variety of sports that some would like to emulate.

Tracts that work the best are short, and to the point, since most people are in a hurry, it has to be something that gets their attention quickly and hold it. Full color and glossy has the ability to instill a greater value that might prevent them from being discarded prematurely.

Some resemble small comic books that are perfect for where the individual has a few minutes to read it. Like at a bus stop, in the waiting room at the doctor's office, or while they are waiting for their car at the car wash. These work especially well with young people.

There are many great strategies for the distribution of tracts. In almost every city, there are large concerts or events. You don't have to pay the fees just to get inside to pass a tract. Just station two people at every exit as the event lets out; give out the pamphlet and cheerfully comment, "Thanks for coming, see you next time." You'll not only have them standing in line to get one, they'll thank you as they pass. On the first weekend the Hollywood subway opened, we took one hundred and fifty people on the subway to go witnessing. While coming up the escalator, I saw a young lady at the top, handing patrons tracts and saying, "Jesus loves you." I only saw two people take one, and none even looked at her. When I reached the top, I suggested she try, "Thanks for riding the red line." She just stared at me, so I repeated, "Just try it." As the next group of riders exited the train and proceeded up the escalator, everyone took one, and most thanked her.

Tracts can be a tool to open a conversation with somebody when you can't think of any other way. In the past, we printed a tract that read on the front, "What has God ever done for you?" You can hand it to someone and ask, "Has God ever done anything for you?" No matter how they respond, it's the beginning of a conversation. The inside of this tract simply shows a close up of Jesus hanging on the cross—No words inside. A picture is worth a thousand words. On the back is a short statement and a prayer if/or when the individual is ready to take the plunge.

Choosing the right tract for the right situation can make a big difference. Another one we produced was titled, *Earthquake Preparedness, Are You Ready?* The inside said, "You have a flashlight, radio, food, water, and extra batteries, but what if you are one of the fatalities, are you ready to meet your Maker? One night in the middle of an outreach, we had a small earthquake. I came in the next morning and said, "Guess which tract is going to work the best today?" It was true, no matter who we offered that tract to that day, they gladly took a copy. There is nothing like death or a crisis to bring someone in touch with eternal issues. We received a phone call from a lady who got one of the Earthquake tracts. She left a message, "Hello, I got a piece of your literature the other day, and I was here for the Northridge earthquake, and I realized I'm not ready, could I talk with someone?"

If you think it is intimidating sharing your faith with someone, maybe you should become a phantom evangelist. That's someone who carries tracts and leaves them everywhere they go but doesn't let anyone see them do it.

A lot of people are just too afraid to carry on a conversation or feel they just don't know enough about God's Word to carry on a good conversation, but still don't want to be left out of the game. This is the job for you.

If you work in an office, you could be the last one to leave one night, but before you walk out, put a tract on everyone's desk, including your own. Then come in five minutes late the next morning and act a little surprised to find this on your desk and casually ask who put it there. They will think there is more than one Christian working there.

Another wonderful way to become known in an office environment is to place your Bible on your desk and put a couple of file folders on top of it. I know your first reaction is, "Why would you want to cover it up if you are trying to become known in your office?" Because you don't want to seem as though you are advertising. You don't even have to read it at lunch either. Just pick it up as you leave for the night. You will be amazed how quickly they'll see it, and since you aren't pushy, they will start the conversation, not you. And they will probably come to you for prayer when they have a crisis.

I also think this is a perfect opportunity for high school students who are a little concerned about peer pressure or are looking for some creative ways to get the information out.

The halls in a school are usually lined with lockers, and even though they may look like ventilation louvers to you, they look like a mail slot to me. A student can get a hall pass during class time, then deliver a tract in every locker, and if yours is in this group, make sure you put one in yours, as well. When classmates start discussing the fact that they got one, you can produce yours, too, and comment on it very innocently. This will produce feedback that will give you insight on where they are at with the Lord, which might help you minister to them at a later date.

Students have a great opportunity to become creative with tracts. You could go to the library, pick up a book, discover this isn't the book you were looking for, slip a tract in it, and put it back on the shelf. Or go to the magazine rack, pull off Sports Illustrated, swimsuit edition, and fill this one full of tracts for the next pervert, I mean, next student to pick up.

I think I created a monster one year with the next idea. Go the restroom, pull out a bunch of T.P. and every two feet back-roll a tract into the roll. What else do they have to do while you're in there? Read the graffiti on the walls? I got an e-mail back from a youth pastor of a young man who caught this vision and thought this was a funny way to witness and have developed a T.P. ministry. Everywhere he goes, he's putting tracts in toilet paper rolls. A little creativity can go a long way.

The reusable tract is a Christian t-shirt. I think students ought to wear one, at least one day a week. The athletes or cheerleaders wear their outfits on Fridays or game days, all the Christian kids should pick one day a week, and all wear them on that day. You don't have to witness, just make a statement. Start a reverse peer pressure.

Don't be flustered if someone throws a tract down without reading it. There was a young man in Hollywood whose life had come crashing down around his ears. In his disgust, he sat on a curb with his forearms bridging his knees. When frustration and sadness finally overcame him, his head dropped, and he began to cry. Moments later, his eyes still flooded with tears, he opened them only to see a tract in the gutter between his feet. He picked it up, read it, and because the contents so fit his situation, he thought it was divine intervention, so he gave his life to Christ right there on the street.

A man from Houston, Texas called The Oasis one day, "I picked up this little piece of paper on the street that asked a question, 'What Has God Ever Done For You?' and I found your number. It made me start to think about how many good things He has done for me. But I have really messed things up in my life. I'm about to lose my marriage and my career. I want God to save me and my marriage." The Heavenly Counselor used that little piece of paper to get his attention and to connect him with someone who could pray for him.

One of the most bizarre stories I have ever heard was about a mountain climber. My understanding is that their climbing boots are both expensive and personal. This young man had worn out the soles of these boots, and instead of replacing them, he decided to have them resoled. Now, after having worn out the second set while climbing, he took off his boots to rub his sore feet. While examining his boots, he bent the toe back to reveal that the sole of one boot had cracked, and he could see something with writing on it below the sole. He began to pick at this piece of paper until he was able to remove it from his boot. It was a tract that the Christian shoe repairman had sewn into his boot. He read it, saw his need for Christ, and on that mountaintop, he asked Jesus into his life.

Conclusion

In Mathew 13:24–30, Jesus uses the parable of the farmer who planted his crop of wheat, but when it came up, it was full of tares. When confronted by his ranch hands, he instantly knew what had happened. An enemy had done this.

Anytime you see the words "heaven is like," stop! Don't just breeze over it and think you've got the gist of it. God always uses analogies that are the closest thing in our human experience to explain His heavenly mysteries. This story is no different. Except for this time, He explains it plainly in verses 36–43.

> *...He who sows the good seed is the Son of Man.*
> *The field is the world, and the good seeds are the*
> *sons (and daughters) of the kingdom...*
> (Matthew 13:37–38 NKJV)

Why us and not His word? Other places in Scripture the good seeds are His words. But here He says it's us.

Why? I believe it's because we are the embodiment of all that He's been trying to do with us since Genesis. We are called, anointed, empowered with His Spirit. We have accepted Him and tasted of the goodness of God. We have the ability to share with more than words, but in deeds, as well. We can do so much that the Word alone can't do. We can have compassion for people because we have experienced so many trials in our own lives; we know what they are going through. Our stories exemplify what God can do with a willing vessel. We are able to teach and instruct and pray in the blessings of God. We can go where the Bible can't because the word of God isn't on us, but in us. We can lay hands on the sick and see them recover. We can do this all over the world simultaneously. Anything we ask Him for will be done so that the Father will be glorified. We are capable of all this and more if we would do just one thing... Just believe it and walk in it.

In my life, I've been an adrenalin junky. I've been into skydiving and scuba diving, street bikes, dirt bikes, and auto racing—Anything that would give me a rush. But NOTHING compares to God using me to touch and save a life. There hasn't been anything more rewarding than helping someone discover Jesus.

I will close with this story. Years ago, a friend and I were driving from Denver back to Southern California. I contracted a crazy flu that put me in a hospital in Phoenix, Arizona. When I was well enough to travel, but still goofy from the strong drugs they had me on, we were about halfway to the California border when we came on an accident that was just happening about an eighth of a mile in front of us. We couldn't see what happened, but we could see a cloud of dust and brake lights were coming on.

This was out in the middle of nowhere—This a place where lizards and rattlesnakes had to be counseled for loneliness and rejection.

Kenny, my friend, instinctively swerved off onto the shoulder and drove up to the scene of the accident. A car had flipped over and threw the occupants out onto the freeway right before we arrived. Kenny stopped the car, and we both jumped out. Kenny ran over to an elderly looking man on the left, and I ran over to a young lady on the right. She looked to be in her early to mid-twenties and looked to be about eight months pregnant. She was conscious and moaning a bit. I knew some basic first aid, so immediately started looking her over. I was looking for compound fractures, severe bleeding, or head injury. I couldn't find anything seriously wrong. She had a loose-fitting skirt, so I could see her whole backside was pretty raw from sliding on the asphalt.

I said, "Ma'am, I can't see anything seriously wrong with you, but your backside is pretty skinned up, and I'm sure you're going to start hurting soon. In short, shallow breaths, she cried, "It's hard to breathe." It didn't take a seven-year medical degree to figure that the baby had shifted and was cramping her breathing. I made her as comfortable as I could and then said, "I can't think of a time that somebody needs Jesus more than a time like this. Do you know Him? Do you have any relationship with Him?"

"No, will you pray for me?"

"Of course, I will. Would you like to receive Him into your life while I'm at it?"

"Yes."

So, right there in the middle of the desert, in the middle of the freeway, I led this young lady to Jesus. Moments later, she died in my arms.

A nurse came just before the end. She said her lungs had collapsed. She drowned in her own saliva.

I got up off the ground and turned to look at all the stopped traffic. Car doors open, drivers standing to the sides of their cars, some with arms crossed, trying to see what was going on.

What would you do? You might think, *Well, I have no authority in this situation. What can I do?* Neither did I, but I took a chance, and I did what I could. I couldn't save her mortal life, but I helped save her eternal life. And the elderly guy? He was already gone. At least one of them had one more opportunity to receive Jesus, and she didn't waste it.

Now make *Your Story Matter*. The harvest is ripe, and the Lord needs you to take your position as His Ambassador, a Fisher of Men, the Salt and Light of the world to reach those in your sphere of influence.

Your Story Matters Discussion Group Workbook

Chapter 1
Who Are These Smiley, Happy People?

1. Discuss the advantages and disadvantages of low or no pressure witnessing.
2. Discuss some of the signs someone may be searching for spiritual significance.
3. How could you be helpful to a new believer?

Chapter 2
211 for Someone's 911

1. What is the 2-1-1 Technique?
2. What stories could I share that could help someone else?
3. Practice the 2-1-1 Technique this week?

Chapter 3
Knees Knocking and Teeth Chattering... Just Do It

1. Matthew 28:19–20 is called the Great Commission. Why?
2. What is the number one reason why people don't share their faith?
3. What is the percentage of Christians who have never led anyone to Christ?
4. What will help you to overcome the fear?

Chapter 4
Power Up with the Helper

1. Who is our Helper? Why was it an advantage for Jesus to go back to the Father according to John 16:7–8?

2. According to John 14:12, Jesus says we can do greater things than He did. How is that possible? Describe some of the greater works.

Chapter 5
The Nudge

1. What does Ron mean by "The Nudge"?
2. How can a "word" from God help in a conversation?
3. Discuss Ron's experience with speaking Ukrainian?
4. How does a miracle help open up someone to talk? Tell the story of what happened at Chad's Bar.

Chapter 6
Starting the Conversation

1. How did Jesus start a conversation in John 5 with a woman and of another race, which was almost unheard of in those days?
2. According to Proverbs 11:30, what does a wise person do? What does "wise" mean in this context?
3. Read Romans 5:8 and discuss how God feels about those who are a sinner.
4. Is it best to start conversations with spiritual matters immediately? If not, how?
5. After making a few statements, what is the best way to end? Why?

6. List the six tips to help in conversing with others.

Chapter 7
The Content of Conversations—Share Your Story

1. Is it necessary to quote a lot of Scriptures?
2. What is Christianese? Give some examples. Why should we avoid using these words?
3. What did Ron mean by "dating God"? How do you use this analogy to demonstrate God's love?
4. What does Ron mean by "seed planters"? Have you failed if you do not pray a salvation prayer with the person?
5. Practice giving a simple explanation of the Gospel.

Chapter 8
Equipping the Saints

1. Explain the analogy of becoming a professional baseball player as it relates to our being a witness for Christ.
2. Discuss what is meant in Ephesians 4:11–12. Who are the coaches?
3. According to 2 Timothy 4:5, each of us has been given a job. What is that?
4. According to 2 Corinthians 5:18, what kind of ministry has God given us?

5. God calls us _____ on this earth in 2 Corinthians 5:20.

6. Discuss:

   a. What that looks like in your daily life.

   b. According to John 14:12, Jesus says that we can do greater things than He did. How is that possible? Describe some of the greater works you've seen or heard of.

   c. John 15:16 tells us we have been "ordained". What does that mean as a layperson?

   d. John 14, 15, and 16 Jesus tells us six different times whatever you need, I will give it to you. Find those six verses and share in what context they are in. What do you need from God to be His ambassador?

Chapter 9
Who Me? An Undercover Agent?

1. What does Ron mean when he calls us Undercover Agents? How can you be an undercover agent in your world?

2. Discuss how we should respond at work as "being a witness".

3. Discuss how Colossians 3:12–14 tells us what to wear.

4. In John 17:21, is Jesus saying we are all to be exactly alike? What area should we be "alike"?

5. We are called _____, no longer _____ by Jesus. Discuss how this helps us in ministering to others (John 15:15).

6. Luke 6:32 tells that even sinners love those who love them. Give the steps to begin ministering to those who need Jesus.

7. Name some of the people who are in your sphere of influence and how you might be able to start reaching out to them.

Chapter 10
Be a "Souldier" Doing Warfare

1. Why is spiritual warfare important?

2. Discuss 2 Corinthians 4:4. What needs to be done to people's eyes?

3. Who are we wrestling with according to 2 Corinthians 10:4?

4. The battle for the souls of men and women are fought and won in our _____ _____.

5. What are the two Greek words for power? Explain the difference in them.

6. What weapon did Jesus use against satan?

Chapter 11
Leaving Tracks with Tracts

1. If you are timid but still want to share your faith, what is another method you could use?
2. What are the most effective kinds of tracts?
3. What are the advantages of being a "phantom evangelist".

Biography Sketch of Ron Radachy

You are to go into all the world and preach the
Good News to everyone, everywhere.

(Mark 16:15 TLB)

Ron and Judy Radachy co-direct The Oasis of Hollywood, a multi-faceted ministry founded in the heart of Hollywood in 1979. They oversee their staff and a variety of programs including:

- Oasis Youth, which meets on Friday nights as an outreach to marginalized urban youth and Tuesday night as a Bible study and youth service.
- Kidz Klubs, which are high energy children's church in public schools.
- Winter and summer camps.

- Special holiday outreaches—Backpack and school supplies event, Thanksgiving turkey and food deliveries, Jesus Birthday parties.
- Hollywood Mission Trip, where Oasis has hosted over 6,600 teens and adults during spring break and summer to receive training in sharing their faith and given opportunities for practical application.

Judy graduated from Christ for the Nations Bible Institute and now serves as an Executive Presbyter for the Alumni Ministers Fellowship. Ron was trained "hands on" for street evangelism with *Soldiers for Jesus Ministries*. Ron and Judy were instrumental in establishing and serving on the steering committee for *The National Streets Ministries Conference* for twelve years. Their best qualifications to minister in Hollywood are a willing spirit and a compassionate heart.

They have appeared on many radio talk shows, such as Dr. Dobson's talk show, as well as CBN (Christian Broadcasting Network), TBN (Trinity Broadcasting Network), and Daystar Network. They regularly speak to churches and at conferences, challenging them to be "Jesus' Body—His hands, His shoulders, His feet—to a hurting and broken world around them."

Both Ron and Judy have teaching CD's available to those who want to be used and stretched by God to influence their cities, and Oasis of Hollywood videos can be found on YouTube.

Ministry Endorsements

Ron and Judy have really made a difference in the world. If anybody's ever blazed a trail and been pioneers in this greater Los Angeles area, they have. Their integrity is just known worldwide. But most of all, they have been our friends, and we love and admire them. They are my heroes.

—Tommy Barnett
Pastor Emeritus of Phoenix First Assembly
Co-Founder of the Los Angeles Dream Center

Ron and Judy are servants of the highest caliber as they love and give unselfishly to those around them to bring the light and life of Jesus in Hollywood. Oasis deserves mission status, for there is not a part of this world where there are missionaries that are more faithfully penetrating the darkness than the Radachy's are.

—Jack Hayford
Chancellor of Kings Seminary
Pastor Emeritus Church on the Way
Former International President of Foursquare

Ron and Judy Radachy have dedicated their lives to reach the lost and hurting of Hollywood. Their determination through difficult times in a difficult place is a testimony of faithfulness. God has called them to a strategic mission field, and their efforts are making a difference.

—David L. Meyer
CEO World Outreach for Joyce Meyer Ministries

People ask me the question, "Who are some of the heroes today of street ministry?" Immediately, I think of Ron and Judy Radachy! All these years on the streets of Hollywood, ministering to some of the most troubled youth in all of America, making a difference every single day. Two warriors who have been fighting for the hearts and minds of people... that's what Oasis of Hollywood is all about!

—Matthew Barnett
Pastor The Dream Center
Los Angeles

Having served in the LAPD for nearly thirty-one years, and in Hollywood Division three times over the course of my career, I can attest to the importance of an organization like the Oasis in creating a refuge for kids. They go pick kids up in communities where I would not venture into unarmed. They teach kids life skills, and they love them.

—Ron Sanchez, LAPD, retd.
Former Captain, Hollywood Division

Ron and Judy have stayed committed to Hollywood for over forty years—through its darkest days and now through its renaissance. I am so grateful for their boundless energy, and their capacity to love, show compassion, and to give without asking for anything in return.

—Kerry Morrison
Former Executive Director
Hollywood Property Owners Alliance

The streets of the nations in the world are teeming with people that are to some simply a nuisance with their begging, stealing, and pimping. Not so to Ron and

Judy and their staff. They see them like Jesus wants all of us to see them—as valuable assets to God, waiting for redemption to become productive, and in turn, to change others.

—Cindy Jacobs
Generals International

I have seen a Hollywood story unfold more dramatic than a screen writer's invention. Here portrayed is true heroism, tenacity, and struggle—inspirational living that transcends time and quietly builds for eternity in the mean streets of the city of dreams.

—John Dawson
President YWAM International

The work of the Oasis in reaching numerous needy young people on the streets of Hollywood remains one of the only rays of hope in an often dreary, despair-filled place. I am both honored and motivated by my partnership with Ron and Judy Radachy as they guide the Oasis, and I am pledged, along with my congregation, to their continued support.

—Lloyd Ogilvie
Former U.S. Senate Chaplain
Former pastor of Hollywood Presbyterian Church

For more information for scheduling Ron or Judy Radachy to minister or to receive the Oasis' monthly printed newsletter or eletter contact them at:

- 323.469.3027
- *Oasis@oasisofhollywood.org*
- P.O Box 1590, Hollywood, CA, 90078
- *www.oasisofhollywood.org*

References

Dunlap, David. n.d. "The Myth of 'Growth' in the Church Growth Movement." Grace Bible Studies. 2020. *http://www.gracebiblestudies.org/Resources/Web/ www.duluthbible.org/g_f_j/TheMythofGrowth.htm.*

"Exousia Meaning in Bible - New Testament Greek Lexicon, Strongs Concordance - King James Version." 2020. Bible Study Tools. 2020. *https://www. biblestudytools.com/lexicons/greek/kjv/exousia.html.*

Jones, Jeffrey. 2019. "U.S. Church Membership Down Sharply in Past Two Decades." Gallup. 2019. *https:// news.gallup.com/poll/248837/church-membership-down-sharply-past-two-decades.aspx.*

"Strong's Number 2450 Hebrew Dictionary of the Old Testament Online Bible with Strong's Exhaustive Concordance, Lexiconcordance.Com." 2020. *Lexicocordance.Come.* 2020. *http://www.lexiconcordance.com/ hebrew/2450.html.*

The Holy Bible: English Standard Version [ESV]. 2007. Wheaton, Ill: Crossway Bibles. Public domain. *https://www.biblegateway.com/versions/ English-Standard-Version-ESV-Bible/#booklist.*

The Holy Bible: King James Version [KJV]. 1999. New York, NY: American Bible Society. Public Domain.

The Holy Bible: Living Bible [TLB]. 1971. Carol Stream, Illinois: Tyndale House Foundation. *https://www. biblegateway.com/versions/The-Living-Bible-TLB/.*

The Holy Bible: New American Standard Bible [NASB]. 1995. The Lockman Foundation. *http://www.lockman. org/nasb/index.php.*

The Holy Bible: New International Version [NIV]. 1984. Grand Rapids: Zonderman Publishing House. *https://www.biblegateway.com/versions/ New-International-Version-NIV-Bible/#booklist.*

The Holy Bible: New Living Translation [NLT]. 2013. Carol Stream: Tyndale House Foundation. Tyndale House Publishers, Inc. *https://www.biblegateway.com/ versions/New-Living-Translation-NLT-Bible/#booklist.*

The Holy Bible: The New King James Version [NKJV]. 1999. Nashville, TN: Thomas Nelson, Inc. *https://www.biblegateway.com/versions/ New-King-James-Version-NKJV-Bible/#booklist.*

"The State of the American Church: Plateaued or Declining The Malphurs Group." 2019. The Malphurs Group. 2019. *https://malphursgroup.com/ state-of-the-american-church-plateaued-declining/.*